OPPORTUNISTIC CHALLENGES:
TEACHING AND LEARNING
WITH ICT

This book is dedicated to
Blanche and Ferdinand Rodrigues

OPPORTUNISTIC CHALLENGES: TEACHING AND LEARNING WITH ICT

SUSAN RODRIGUES
EDITOR

Nova Science Publishers, Inc.
New York

Senior Editors: Susan Boriotti and Donna Dennis
Coordinating Editors: Tatiana Shohov and Jennifer Vogt
Office Manager: Annette Hellinger
Graphics: Wanda Serrano
Editorial Production: Matthew Kozlowski, Jonathan Rose, and Maya Columbus
Circulation: Ave Maria Gonzalez, Vera Popovic and Vladimir Klestov
Communications and Acquisitions: Serge P. Shohov
Marketing: Cathy DeGregory

Library of Congress Cataloging-in-Publication Data
Available upon request.
ISBN 1-59033-351-9

Copyright © 2002 by Nova Science Publishers, Inc.
    400 Oser Ave, Suite 1600
    Hauppauge, New York 11788-3619
    Tele. 631-231-7269   Fax 631-231-8175
    e-mail: Novascience@earthlink.net
    Web Site: http://www.novapubishers.com

CONTENTS

ACKNOWLEDGEMENTS

The editor would like to thank the authors of the various chapters for their willing contributions to this book. The views expressed in this book are those of the authors and do not necessarily reflect the views of their employers. Most of the chapters are based on ideas presented by the authors in other publications and facets of the chapters have appeared in print elsewhere. Every effort has been made to ensure that copyright has not been breached and the editor would be happy to hear from anyone whose rights they have unwittingly infringed.

The editor would like to thank the people who helped create the images found within the book or the packages used to collect the data, people who were working with the authors during the research process. Thanks also to C Colla, Dr M Livett, Dr A Marks, B Rodrigues, F Rodrigues, Dr G Rogers, N Wong, and S Young, for various comments and suggestions.

ABOUT THE CONTRIBUTORS

Dr. Susan Rodrigues

Dr Rodrigues is the Director, Institute of Science Education in Scotland. Previous to that she was the Director, Initial Teacher Education at the University of Stirling. She has been an academic at the University of Durham and the University of Melbourne, she has also worked as a senior research officer at the National Foundation for Education Research (England)and prior to that taught in schools in England and New Zealand. Her research interests lie in the area of context and the role of ICT in learning science.

Paul Edwards

Paul Edwards has spent the last seven years working to integrate technology with the higher education curriculum. His Master of Education thesis addressed the lack of consideration for contemporary theories of learning when using technology in a teaching environment. He is currently the Research Support Officer for the Melbourne Advanced Research Computing Centre, University of Melbourne. Email: paule@unimelb.edu.au.

Dr. Mary Ainley

Dr. Mary Ainley is a Senior Lecturer in the Department of Psychology at the University of Melbourne, Australia. Her areas of interest are in Developmental and Educational Psychology and include the study of motivational processes such as curiosity, interest, engagement and students' achievement goals. Current research projects involve using interactive multimedia to identify ways that students engage with specific learning tasks and how motivation influences learning outcomes. E-mail: maryda@unimelb.edu.au

Jon Pearce

Jon Pearce is a Senior Lecturer in the Department of Information at the University of Melbourne. He has a background in physics education and lectured in physics at the university before moving to Information Systems. He is currently researching the roles that interactivity and multimedia play in promoting learning in on-line environments. His email address is: jonmp@unimelb.edu.au

John S. Murnane

He is a former primary teacher with a long standing interest in the use of computer and communication technologies in education. He teaches preservice and graduate teachers in these areas. His main research interests are problem solving in a computing environment, programming languages for teaching, the use of the Internet in education and the home and the sociology of Internet games.

Albert Ip

Mr. Albert Ip has a long history of working in learning technology. In he designed MonNet, which was able to broadcast the image from a teacher's computer to the students' workstations using a low cost overriding mechanism. In 1986, Albert and his students designed, and built a Local Area Network for Apple II computers. He later shifted his focus towards software implementations. In 1994, he had designed TeleNex, an English language teacher support system for the University of Hong Kong incorporating hypertext database, automatic generation of test items, online asynchronous conferencing and English corpus database. One of Mr. Ip's latest work is Fablusi, a Role-Play Simulation Generator, which is based on his research on scalable learning architecture for Internet. Albert is also a frequent writer on the learning technology and pedagogical implications of learning technology, including issues related to resource discovery, learning objects and metadata. He is currently, the Managing Director of Digital Learning Systems P/L, a company that provides online learning solutions to educational and training institutions.

INTRODUCTION

Susan Rodrigues

Over the last few years there has been a lot of thought and finance invested in promoting various Information Communication Technology (ICT) initiatives in education environments. Many of the initiatives are aimed at developing more flexible systems of learning with a core aim to provide the learner with more choice, in terms of what, where and how they learn. To a certain extent the rationale for these initiatives is to increase efficiency and effectiveness in learning benefit. But to date, much of the rhetoric surrounding the promotion of ICT has not always resulted in delivered learning benefit. In the past it could have been argued that the delivered benefit did not materialize because there were insufficient resources available. But now, the resource levels in learning environments are significant. The reasons for not fulfilling the anticipated potential may now be due to a lack of understanding in how these technologies should have been designed or it may be due to the technologies being used inappropriately and hence less effectively. If we hope to maximise the potential of ICT then we need to understand the potential of what is available and we need to consider the opportunities that exist in the eye of the designer, the teacher and the learner.

A key aim of this book is to signal some of the challenges and opportunities that we face in designing and using appropriate technologies within various learning environments. I wanted to add to the discussion on the development of effective ICT systems and products for various learning environments. Clearly this is a demanding remit for a small book, because it requires the authors to make transparent their understanding of the users, computers and organisations' remits, purposes and interactions. However, I felt that I knew sufficient people who were engaged in exactly that, people who were trying to unpack the way ICT is used, and people who were trying to demonstrate how the ICT could be used effectively. The authors within this book report on their explorations and perceptions of the nature and relationships between interactions connecting users, computers and organisations, and in so doing they describe some of the challenges and opportunities we face as we move to include more and more ICT in teaching and learning.

A key intention of the book is to report on the work of several researchers and product developers engaged in investigating the potential of ICT in learning environments in terms of users, computers and organisation. These researchers and product developers will bring with them their personal pet theories and their professional views. These theories and views should stimulate debate about effective ICT use in learning environments. Though I acknowledge that there is no one view of learning, in recent times I have subscribed to a view of learning that includes an awareness of the social and cognitive dimension of the learning processes as well as a consciousness of the idea of organisational learning. Not surprisingly therefore, in this book, when we review the effectiveness of ICT use in learning environments we see numerous challenges and opportunities in terms of the social, cognitive and organisational dimensions. The challenges and opportunities reported in this book depend on the interpretation of the learning process and as such the chapters reflect each author's views of learning. At the core of the majority of the chapters there is a view of learning that would fit well within the Constructivist School of thought which fragments into various interpretations (such as social constructivism, personal constructivism, radical constructivism). It should be noted, however, that it is not the sole view of learning represented in the book. There are brief forays into Enactivism and Symbolic Interactionism, or Information processing views of learning. This is deliberate, as it is not the intention of the book to simply signal the challenges and opportunities in light of one particular view of learning.

Much of the rhetoric promotes the use of ICT as a tool to enhance teaching. Indeed, much of the research documents uptake of ICT resources in classrooms, some of it reports on the use of specific tools and some of it reports on teacher professional development in the use of ICT. There are periodical reports of evidence documenting the benefits in using ICT. To a certain extent much of what has been documented views the inclusion of various products/software as unproblematic in terms of facilitating learning. It is assumed that the inclusion of these products/software will result in benefit for the learner and enhanced classroom practice and in some cases these benefits are reported. Enhancement is seen in terms of increased pupil motivation, better conceptual understanding, the acquisition of informed views, positive learning outcomes and the development of inquiry skills. In this book we explore some of these notions in more detail, but we also consider the extent to which the currently available software/products construct or hinder this enhancement.

There are two key themes within the book: the influence of learning theory on design and the influence of design on learning. The first section of the book discusses some implications for design of e-learning environments. The second section of the book concentrates on the influence of design on learning, and reports on investigations into the nature of interactivity and its impact on student learning. The authors in this book report on their analysis of challenges and opportunities in terms of pupil learning and in terms of software development.

We begin with a chapter that situates our current e-learning curve in the experiences of other technology driven learning curves. Paul Edwards provides a narrative that signals some of the lessons provided through the introduction of learning technologies used in the past. In his chapter, Edwards encourages us to reflect on the demands and challenges, opportunities and goals made available by the use of ICT, in the context of how we interpreted and adopted other distance learning mediums for educational purposes. He briefly reviews various learning theories and documents the impact these theories have had on our interpretation of the goals and values of ICT in education. Edwards then describes the use of television and radio in the promotion of education goals. By encouraging us to reflect on currently advocated ICT fitness for classroom purposes, Edwards frames the discussion that follows in the remaining chapters.

In chapter four I explore some of the challenges education researchers and software designers face when trying to construct software influenced by learning theory. I explore the process of collaborative work, and focus on the influence and expectation of experience and group members' background on the development of a CDROM for school chemistry. Vygotsky's notion of ZPD (1962) refers to the zone in which learning occurs in the presence of scaffolding by a more informed other. In the development of educational software there is a need for reciprocal support as the informed other is expert in their own domain and novice in the other. The software designer would be an expert in the field of design and relatively inexperienced in the area of learning theory, while the educator is unlikely to be conversant with software development but more familiar with education learning theory. Hence the creation of a Chemistry CDROM that takes into account learning theory would require scaffolding to be provided by both parties. I illustrate some of the complexities and multiple stages of research and engagement that exist when software engineers and education experts work collaboratively to develop a CDROM for school chemistry. The overlapping of ZPD, and the existence of novice in one domain and expert in another has repercussions for the development of software, mainly because the participants share common terms but have different meanings for these terms and because they also have different agendas to address. Hence the construction of the CDROM is significantly influenced by different interpretations. The chapter reinforces the centrality of social interaction in the development of effective resource materials for learners.

In chapter three, John Murnane looks at the world of simulations. Murnane makes a case for more explicit simulation systems. He suggests that simply providing students and teachers with access to control of a simulation, without understanding, or even an awareness, of the omissions, simplifications, approximations, analogies or reality that underpins the simulation, will lead to the user constructing inappropriate conclusions and constructs. He suggests that information underpinning the development of the simulation should be made explicit. In that way, those operating the simulation are aware of its limitations with respect to reality. Hence when running, for example, a simulation of a nuclear reactor, the user manipulates inputs, observes outputs and draws conclusions without any real understanding of the omissions, simplifications, approximations, analogies employed by the programme designer. As a consequence they may draw inadvisable and inappropriate conclusions. Murnane suggests that information on the simulation in terms of the 'guesstimates' made are rarely, if at all, provided by commercial simulator providers, yet it is a significant part of the decision making and conclusion drawing process, and as a consequence it is a significant part of the learning process.

The inclusion of Constructivist ideas in ICT use has long been debated. Some propose that either the technology incorporates Constructivist ideas or the technology is used in a Constructivist environment. Ip's description of a Role Play Simulation environment is an attempt to combine both these aspects. The philosophy underpinning the use of simulations as pedagogical tools relies on an idea that experience is the basis of learning. Albert Ip, in chapter five explores this notion of experience, but Ip also suggests that these technology driven opportunities should encourage us to refresh our pedagogical beliefs. He questions online training/learning models in which learners work alone with a computer. He suggests that if real, rather than virtual experience is impossible, expensive or dangerous, then a discourse virtual environment may encourage learning. The chapter describes a strategy that seeks to integrate Constructivist ideas with online technology potential. Ip articulates an underlying pedagogical design for a Role Play Simulation environment. He suggests that the Role Play Simulation environment is a form of online problem based learning where participants adopt 'roles' and participate in a role play online. Ip signals moderation issues stemming from capturing and utilising the learning opportunities while engaging those involved in the Role Play Simulation environment. What Ip describes is the integration of communication and computation in order to open up new potential and opportunity.

In chapter 6, I report on a study where tertiary Physics students used web based simulations and data loggers. I report on an investigation that I undertook with Jon Pearce and Michelle Livett into the way data loggers and simulations helped and hindered students learning physics, learning to do physics and learning about physics. I report on an aspect of that project (for further details of the project see Rodrigues, Pearce and Livett, 2001). I focus on the students' mindfulness and mindlessness, terms proposed by Langer (1993), when tertiary students work with dataloggers and web based simulations. I view their experience of these technologies as part of their social negotiation of meaning for the science they are learning. In school science lessons, or tertiary science laboratories, the student's goal, the situation in which they find themselves and their determination of the adequacy of their existing understandings are critical factors in determining their mindfulness and mindlessness. To what extent does the students' use of ICT affect their mindfulness and mindlessness and hence the adequacy of their existing science understandings? The chapter describes the learning strategies used by tertiary students working on a first-year physics laboratory exercise involving the analysis of experiments on the topic of motion using either a data logger or video analysis of simulations. The chapter highlights the crucial nature of learning activities and the critical importance of designing carefully researched activities if we are to expect students to engage mindfully with the technology.

Engagement in mindful activity relies to a certain extent on the integration of communication and computation. The significant uptake of CDROMS for use in science classroom practice suggests a perception that communication and computation have best been integrated in CDROMS. At least one of the parties engaged in human computer dialogue must have an intrinsic incentive to interact. While a computer has been programmed to respond, the human partner in the dialogue must show initiative. This initiative will depend on the user's disposition toward learning. This disposition will have a significant influence on the impact of ICT on learning. It is my contention that we need to pay more consideration to learner disposition if we want to encourage effective and independent work with CDROMs in classrooms. Chapter 7 draws on findings from two projects that investigated student disposition toward types of features commonly found in Chemistry CDROMS. I describe students' perceptions of these various facets in terms of their utility. In one project I investigated students' approaches to working with an award winning CDROM when given open access for a limited time. The other project involved an investigation into video/animation facets commonly found in CDROMS and it employed a custom designed package (provided by Mary Ainley) which tracked students' engagement. Both projects illustrate some factors that influence student disposition to explore aspects of the CDROM. The tracking of students in one project indicated that students were not disposed toward being comprehensive navigators while direct observation and video analysis from the other project indicated that students were not disposed to access unfamiliar topics and they were most interested in the quiz section. Some of the reasons given for this stem from cognitive overload, ease of navigation and motivation.

In the final chapter Mary Ainley and Jon Pearce report on an ongoing investigation into how interactivity affects learning outcomes. They are interested in investigating ways that interactivity found in ICT materials contribute to learning. They are also interested in the nature of student motivation and engagement when ICT is used for the delivery of specific learning content. Their methodology closely monitors students' behaviour within specific learning environments and they use a more developed methodology to that described in chapter 6, where they use the technology as a window into students' engagement with particular learning content delivered through ICT. Ainley and Pearce describe the learning sequence adopted by students faced with a web based activity. The students were first year undergraduate Psychology students, the majority of whom were not studying physics. Ainley and Pearce suggest that a crucial part of the effectiveness of interactivity in ICT is whether the student wants to understand the new information. In terms of performance goals Ainley and Pearce showed that students demonstrated a different relationship with learning. Students who endorsed this type of goal were concerned to do and score well on assessments and perform well to meet social expectations. Ainley and Pearce's sample show that performance goals were negatively related to achievement on two types of learning measure. They do suggest that this may be due to the fact that these were not Physics students. They also suggest that while an interactive module within a well designed learning sequence can support learning if students actually engage with it, not all students come to their learning with goals and purposes compatible with this learning mode.

The book does not set out to reveal best practice or demonstrate consensus views on how to use ICT. Instead, I have invited several colleagues to present some of their views regarding the opportunities available and the challenges we face if ICT is to influence learning rather than deliver teaching, or for that matter, simply entertain the learner. Human computer interaction involves communication and rules, and now, if we want to engage in the digital age, we need to surrender our analog way of using rules and take ownership of the communication process. The aim of this book is simply to promote discussion on the challenges and opportunities we face during this period of transition, with a view to disseminating our understandings and awareness of some social and cognitive factors that influence the effectiveness of ICT.

REFERENCES

Langer, E.J (1993) A Mindful Education. *Educational Psychologist*, 28, (1) pp. 43-50

Rodrigues, S., Pearce, J., and Livett, M. (2001) Using Video-Analysis or Data loggers During Practical work in first year physics, *Educational Studies*, 27, (1) pp31-44`

Vygotsky, L. S. (1962) *Thought and language.* Cambridge, Mass: MIT Press.

LESSONS FROM THE PAST: EFFECTIVE LEARNING USING NEW TECHNOLOGIES

Paul Edwards

"Before you become too entranced with gorgeous gadgets and mesmerizing video displays, let me remind you that information is not knowledge, knowledge is not wisdom, and wisdom is not foresight. Each grows out of the other, and we need them all."

Arthur C. Clarke

INTRODUCTION

ICT is the latest example of technology being integrated into education. Films, television, · radio, audiocassette, specialized AV facilities, and the calculator, are all examples of technologies which already have been integrated into education with varying degrees of success. Why have some technologies succeeded while others have not? Is the success (or otherwise) of a technology a result of the features specific to that technology? Can these considerations be applied to ICT to increase its effectiveness in education? What teaching methods and techniques can be used to achieve good learning outcomes using ICT?

To answer these questions, it is essential to have an understanding both of how people learn and to identify good practice in instructional design. This chapter focuses on good practice in instructional design.

LEARNING AND INSTRUCTIONAL DESIGN

Instructional design encompasses the design of the instructional content; the manner in which the instruction will be presented; and the use of teaching aides to facilitate knowledge transfer and retention. High quality instructional design should lead to a more successful transfer of knowledge and construction of the knowledge base.

Knowledge construction is the assumed mechanism that guides the change of knowledge in many theories of learning. Learners are actively involved in the learning process and construct their knowledge base from previously acquired knowledge (Lai, 1989) and experience (Riding & Buckle, 1987). Magidson defines constructivism such that "in order for someone to learn something, he or she must actively process that knowledge by relating it to previous knowledge" (1992, pp. 2-3). Learning experiences need not add extra information to the knowledge base; rather they may cause existing links within the knowledge base to be altered or removed to more accurately represent the new information. An ill-structured knowledge base can lead to obstacles for concept mastery, including a lack of transferability of concepts to novel situations, and an inability to generalize the concepts learned (Spiro, Feltovich, Jacobson and Coulson, 1991).

Learning is a social activity (Kozma, 1994), as well as a set of cognitive constructs and theories, and this should be considered when thinking about instructional design. Learning is an active process of constructing knowledge, "whereby the learner strategically manages the available cognitive resources to create new knowledge by extracting information from the environment and integrating it with information already stored in memory" (Kozma, 1991, p. 179). A key factor in successful learning is therefore the construction of semantic networks – accurate representations of real world systems by the learner (Kozma, 1994) – and integrating these into the knowledge base. Eisenhart et al (1993) use the example of division of fractions to illustrate semantic networks. The concept behind the division of fractions is thought of as the union of knowledge of fractions and knowledge of division. These two areas of prior knowledge are then linked together to construct a knowledge of the division of fractions. In a properly constructed semantic network, the relationship between ideas represented by the knowledge base allows learners to explain a phenomenon and justify it. Similarly, a new learning experience allows learners to strengthen their understanding of previously learnt concepts by re-arranging their existing knowledge base.

The precise means of knowledge representation and encoding is not known, but it is recognized that individuals do represent knowledge in different ways (for example, Gardner, 1993). Information from the environment, including conversation with other learners and the learner's own reflection is an important part of the learning process. Two key instructional devices to assist in knowledge construction are appropriate metaphors (Kozma, 1994; Marchionini, 1991); and automatization, through which learners automate tasks or concepts thus reducing cognitive overhead in later, related, learning episodes (Heckman, 1993; Cocking & Mestre, 1989; Spiro et al, 1991; Reigeluth & Schwartz, 1989).

Gagné, Briggs and Wager (1992) propose nine key events of instruction: (1) gaining attention; (2) informing the learner of the objective; (3) stimulating the recall of previous learning; (4) presenting the stimulus material; (5) providing the learning guidance; (6) eliciting the performance from the learner; (7) providing feedback about performance assessment; (8) assessing the performance; and (9) enhancing retention and transfer of knowledge. Not all of these events occur in every learning situation; similarly, there may be some learning situations where other, additional, instructional events occur. These nine events of instruction have relevance when considering the role that technology plays in education.

The attention of the learner may be gained by various techniques; initially, appealing to the learner's interests and later through various stimuli changes during the presentation of the course material. Instruction using technology allows many natural stimulus changes: switching attention between the computers, whiteboard, projected display, and group learning (when appropriate) refocuses the learner on the task.

Providing the learner with desired learning outcomes allows the learner to construct an expectation of what learning outcomes should be met by the completion of the instruction. This provides the learner with a focus for the course, as well as allowing self-evaluation of progress to take place. The target audience and context determines how explicitly the desired learning outcomes are stated: for example, "Sesame Street" never explicitly states the desired learning outcomes, whilst the first lecture of a University level course generally includes a handout describing the assessment and learning criteria. In the latter situation, the learner should also be aware of the nature of performance that is used as an indication that learning has occurred.

The learner's prior knowledge can be stimulated through the use of recall and recognition questions. Questions which stimulate previously learnt knowledge to lead to the desired conclusion are suitable to achieve both recall and serve as an introduction for the presentation of new material. This type of questioning places the teacher in the position to provide guidance, as distinct from explicit instruction. This can lead to discovery learning where the learner may gain a deeper understanding of the concept(s) underlying the problem being encountered, which in turn may lead to enhanced retention of the content (Gagné, Briggs, & Wager, 1992).

Recall and recognition questions provide a valuable feedback loop between the teacher and learner. The teacher must assess the answers from the learner to ensure that the questions asked are appropriate. The human teacher can recognize areas where the learner is struggling to grasp concepts, and can adjust the lesson to allow for this lack of understanding. The teacher can also encourage the learner to spend time reflecting on how an answer was derived. The human teacher can also provide lateral input to the learning process by suggesting that the learner consider the concept being learnt in a different context, or by associating it with a previously learnt item of knowledge (actively encouraging the construction of links between nodes in the knowledge base).

A useful strategy to adopt when accounting for individual differences between learners when teaching in this manner is to progressively disclose hints. This avoids frustration on the part of slower learners, and provides the teacher with good feedback on the progress of all learners. This disclosure of hints requires that the question-answer feedback loop have been established between the teacher and the learner.

The presentation of new information to the learner must occur as part of the instructional sequence in a contextually relevant manner. The contextual relevance is determined by considering factors including knowledge construction, and the appropriateness of the information to the example(s) used in the course. The use of multiple examples is important to ensure that the learner has not just learnt that one instance, rather the underlying principles and concepts have been learnt. Gagné, Briggs and Wager relate an instance where "a boy could recognize a vertical position when a pencil was used a test object, but not when a table knife was held in that position." (1992, p. 194).

Once the appropriate stimulus material has been presented, the learner should demonstrate the performance of the desired learning objective. In the context of a syllabus with no formal assessment, this is also an appropriate time to provide the learner with feedback to indicate the degree of success of the performance. Depending upon the context (especially when using ICT), feedback may be automatically provided through the nature of the task to be performed.

When the learner has demonstrated task competency, the teacher must be sure that the performance was both valid (the performance reflects the learning objective) and reliable (no simple memorizing of answers has taken place, and the conditions under which the task was performed were free of distortion). The validity of the task performance is determined by the clarity with which the teacher sets the tasks and the accuracy with which the instructions are followed. The reliability of the performance can be increased by multiple task performances.

To achieve retention of knowledge, regular practice is required. Practice immediately following the instruction is relatively ineffective (Gagné, Briggs, & Wager, 1992). To successfully increase the generality and transferability of the knowledge constructed, the preparation of a number of new tasks in a variety of contexts substantially different from the one in which the task was first presented, is desirable. The variety and novelty of tasks assists in the continuing development of cognitive strategies. This in turn demonstrates the generality of the solution obtained.

After considering the nine events of instruction, the first task facing the instructional designer is to determine the sequence in which the objectives are taught (assuming that the scope of the course content is known) and appropriate learning objectives based on this content are set. The primary concern when determining the ordering of objectives should be the order in which they are best learned; other issues such as a variety of learning outcomes and the application of different teaching and learning styles should be considered later (Gagné, Briggs, & Wager, 1992). A learning environment where each item can be taught in a number of different ways is desirable (Spiro et al, 1991), but achieving this should not come at the expense of the appropriate ordering of objectives, information overload and the lack of automatization

Instructional content should incorporate concepts as well as facts because it is important that students can reason from first principles rather than relying on the application of techniques learnt by rote. The teaching of principles, and emphasizing research and enquiry rather than techniques and facts, is an appropriate approach to adopt when determining the nature of the content in the instructional course (Winn, 1988; Roszak, 1988, as cited in Atkins, 1993; Thurman & Mattoon, 1992). Good teachers tend to teach basic principles and problem solving strategies rather than pure facts (Collins & Stevens, 1982).

A designer must take into account the different levels of prior knowledge relevant to the learning outcomes that each learner possesses (Haag & Grabowski, 1995; Gagné, Briggs, & Wager, 1992). Designing the course using the linking of concepts as the key criteria of sequence assists accommodating different levels of prior knowledge among participants. This allows the more advanced learner to strengthen their existing links, while the less advanced learner can use the same instructional material to construct these links.

A course must be flexible enough to allow the teacher to decide on how best to present the information to construct the learner's knowledge base (Magidson, 1992). A learning environment where the same items can be taught (and hence learned) in a number of different ways is therefore desirable (Spiro et al, 1991). When the learning environment incorporates ICT, the technology may be an enabler or an inhibitor of this flexibility, and this should be considered in the design of the instruction and the selection of technology.

Integrating Technology and Instructional Design

The nature and quality of the software used with ICT should be well considered from the outset. Software does more than allow computers to run; it defines the parameters of the resultant environment (Ullmer, 1992). Therefore, the choice of software as a design decision not only utilizes technology, but also intrinsically defines its role and effectiveness in instruction.

It is common to see new technology placed on top of older, didactic teaching models, where knowledge is viewed as a quantity of abstract self-contained facts and concepts to be delivered to the learner (Ullmer, 1992). Early integration of technology into the design process should overcome this problem. It is important that designers do not separate media from the process of instructional design (Kozma, 1994). A high level of abstraction between the design and the technology means that not all available attributes of media used in the course of instruction may be utilized. The attributes of any medium are defined as its complete capabilities (Kozma, 1994), which encompasses not only audio-visual aspects of media, but also considers issues such as the potential level of interactivity the media can perform.

Learning in a technological environment should support learning (Ullmer, 1992) rather than using the technology as simple page turning devices, where the computer acts as a book, albeit a book which makes sounds and can display high quality graphics. Technology should be used to allow and encourage the learner to question, to not accept facts at face value and to seek challenges, rather than just for rote learning (Ullmer, 1992). Thus technology can provide opportunities for learning new ideas as well as revising and practicing known ideas.

When the instructional designer is aware of the attributes of all media which may be integrated into the instruction, then they can take best advantage of the features each form of media has to offer in achieving each learning objective. Indeed, "there is no one medium which is universally superior to all others for all types of desired outcomes and for all learners" (Gagné, Briggs, & Wager, 1992, p. 210). For example, the learner can more directly form a mental model when presented with dynamic visual information rather than static information (Cognition and Technology Group, 1991), particularly when motion is an essential element of the concept or skill to be learned (Gagné, Briggs, & Wager, 1992). Incorporating video playback facilities (either computer based or controlled through a conventional video tape recorder) into the instruction allows the instructional designer to make better use of media attributes in designing instruction for achieving learning objectives than if media were separated from the design process.

Good computer simulation design recommends the simulation be broken down into various levels with few variables on the first level, progressively increasing in difficulty until the final level is a full complexity simulation of the real world system being modeled (Reigeluth & Schwartz, 1989). This is analogous to "the progressive disclosure of system features and capabilities" as proposed by Marchionini (1991, p.16). Computer Based Training allows the learner to practice the skills learnt during the instructional period (Haag & Grabowski, 1995; Reigeluth & Schwartz, 1989). The techniques used by CDROMs which may be applied when integrating ICT into educational design are: (1) an increasing level of difficulty; (2) time to practice skills; and (3) having enough structure in the course to allow smooth progression, but not so much structure that exploring is discouraged.

The availability of guidance to the learner is an important aspect of good instructional design; either in the form of set tasks or a realizable goal. Little learning occurs when no guidance is given and the learner is left to explore on their own (Haag & Grabowski, 1995), especially in a hypermedia environment, where the learner can easily become confused and indulge in superficial browsing (Ellis, Ford & Wood, 1993). Care should be taken by the course designer, for encouraging discovery learning allows the learner to question facts, seek challenges, and not accept presented facts at face value. To achieve this, designers have to recognize the key elements of the environment to be simulated (Ullmer, 1992).

The producers of "Sesame Street" were effective at applying some of these instructional techniques, plus others, to produce a television programme which resulted in learning outcomes. This included casting the learner in an active role despite the inherent passivity of the television medium. An examination of how the producers of "Sesame Street" were able to overcome limitations in the medium used, may provide useful lessons for educators wishing to incorporate ICT into teaching and learning in the 21st century.

TELEVISION AS A LEARNING TECHNOLOGY

Television was seen as the "next big thing" for education in the 1950s. It would transcend socio-economic factors, and allow the poorest families access to the best educators (Stoll, 1999). There have been some educational benefits derived from television, but "what happened to the great educational boon that was supposed to follow?" (Stoll, 1999, p.118).

Television is, by default, a passive medium. Visual and aural information is broadcast to a room with no active involvement required on the part of the learner. It requires work from the teacher (or parent) to turn the TV watching experience into an active one (Kaplan, 1986). Television allows the learner to view footage of places they would otherwise not see, and docu-dramas can re-create historic events, "as long as children understand that much of what they are watching may have been invented for the program." (Kaplan, 1986, p.43).

The producers of the programme "Sesame Street" set out to achieve sound learning outcomes from watching television. Research conducted in the USA in 1995 showed that people who watched "Sesame Street" regularly as children performed significantly better at high school than did their non- "Sesame Street"-watching counterparts. High school grade point averages increased by 0.052 for every hour of Sesame Street" watched per week (cited in Gladwell, 2000, p.264).

They made the programme colourful and adopted a so-called magazine format, where there was not one single narrative for the episode, but a series of discrete and distinct articles (or segments). Tests run by Lorch and Anderson showed that the maximum time that any segment should run in "Sesame Street" was four minutes, with three minutes being the optimal time period (Gladwell, 2000). This strategy was adopted to conform with the prevailing theory of the time: that pre-schoolers had short attention spans (Lesser, 1974).

Each season of "Sesame Street" had clearly defined educational goals (Lesser & Schneider, 2000). Formative research was performed to ensure that each series reflected the changing and diverse nature of the viewing population, making the material relevant to the population of the time. By this stage, the producers had a framework which seemed to work, so the results from these surveys informed the "Sesame Street" framework. (Lesser & Schneider (2000, pp.31-34) provides a table which documents the range of learning objectives in the "Sesame Street" curriculum.)

The producers acknowledged that there was an element of passivity in the television medium, despite the observation that some children talk to or sing along with the television. They aimed to "encourage active participation through numerous programming devices" (Lesser, 1974, p.83). The devices they employed included swelling music, dramatic pauses, fade in/fade out, freeze-frames, and zoom effects, although excessive use of these effects resulted in children losing interest (Gladwell, 2000). The producers also kept things simple: too much wordplay distracted the viewer from the main aim of the segment (Gladwell, 2000).

Considerable trialling of segments and episodes occurred. Lesser (1974) provides some examples of the elements the producers examined. Multiple levels of meaning were built into the segments, and when the viewer saw the same segment for a second or third time, they would often look for (and find) new meanings. A comparison of spoken words and pictures was performed to see which mode was superior, and it was found that synchronizing multiple input modalities (vision and sound) provided better learning outcomes than either mode by itself.

"Sesame Street" employed cognitive devices consistent with modern learning theory: (1) knowledge construction; (2) consistency; (3) imitation and practice; (4) low noise; and (5) variable pacing.

Knowledge construction was an important philosophy behind many of the techniques used by the producers of "Sesame Street". The viewer got used to the animations and the street scene, but "Sesame Street" also took the viewer to other, non-familiar, places: farms, junkyards, trips on a bus – anywhere that the viewer may not be able to go themselves. The producers acknowledged that these experiences could not replace the physical experience of visiting these places, but that there was benefit in letting the viewer know that these places exist and a basic understanding of what went on there was better than no understanding at all (Lesser, 1974).

The producers of the show thought it important to keep the format consistent (Palmer & Fisch, 2001). The consistent use of visual icons, for example, meant that the viewer knew from experience when they saw the voice balloon that they were going to be learning about letters. Sound, the other cue modality used by television, was also used to similar effect.

Imitation and practice was another cognitive device employed by the show's producers (Lesser, 1974). The same segment would be repeated throughout a week's programming. This had two benefits: first, if the viewer failed to understand the concept of the segment during its first viewing then there is a subsequent opportunity for the learning to take place; and second, repeated viewing provided opportunity to reinforce the concept (Fisch & Truglio, 2001). The viewer would also have the opportunity to practice the content of the segment (spelling of words, letter pronunciation, etc), which may in turn lead to the automatization of the concept, thus reducing cognitive overload for further learning.

"Sesame Street" also reduced the amount of "noise" in the segments (Lesser, 1974). (In this context, "noise" refers to information extraneous to the educational goal for the segment). This meant that the viewer could concentrate on the topic being presented, and not have to use cognitive resources for discriminating what was important from what was not – it was found that viewers of the programme often focussed on the peripheral details rather than the primary concept. There was a motivational reason for reducing noise as well: it was found that "if they [the viewers] couldn't make sense of what they were looking at, they weren't going to look at it" (Gladwell, 2000, p. 101). Noise reduction required the analysis of the educational goal for the segment whilst considering the context in which the goal was going to be presented.

The "Oscar's Blending" segment shows how the analysis was performed to remove noise. In this segment, the muppet Oscar "blended" letters together to make words – "c" and "at" creates the word "cat". Oscar was at the top of the screen; the letters arrived on the bottom of the screen. The producers took photographs of the position of children's eyes, and found that the children were watching the movements of Oscar rather than the words and letters at the bottom of the screen. Minimizing Oscar's movement kept the children watching the letters, and therefore focussed on the task.

There was a deliberate decision to make the segments variably paced. Keeping the segments at the same pace seemed to indicate that the viewer lost interest as the show progressed. By changing the pace of the segments, the show held on to the viewer's attention for a longer period of time (Lesser, 1974). The role of the muppets (such as Grover and Big Bird) was also interesting; Lesser (1974) implies that they were deliberately cast in the role of a facilitator, guiding the viewer, rather than a sage.

SHORT-WAVE RADIO AS A LEARNING TECHNOLOGY

Schools of the Air are correspondence schools where students and teachers get an additional yet fundamental opportunity to interact, via short-wave radio. Students registered with Schools of the Air are generally children who live in remote regions of Australia and other countries. Australia alone has over twenty different Schools of the Air, most of which are descended from earlier state based correspondence schools for rural and remote students set up between 1906

(Queensland) and 1979 (Northern Territory). The short-wave radio was introduced in the 1950s.

The Schools of the Air use technology in a novel yet vital way. The majority of the work from the schools of the air is in the form of paper-based correspondence work. This model requires and assumes the presence of a home tutor (Daws, 1999) – usually a parent – who is able to assist the students with their work. The short-wave radio is used to supplement the materials provided, and allows the teacher to work through any areas of difficulty with the students. The amount of formal time on the radio varies from school to school, but is in the range of thirty to ninety minutes per weekday, depending on class size and atmospheric conditions (Rogers, 2000). Adverse atmospheric conditions mean that communications frequently are one way (for example, a student may hear the teacher, but the teacher cannot hear the student). As a result other students acted as relays (Rogers, personal communication, 2001). The short-wave radio is also used by the students for socializing; it is the only way in which they can regularly communicate with children their own age.

Students are sent course materials on a regular (usually term) basis. The course materials are a mix of paper notes, filmstrips/videos, audiotapes, and special kits for science experiments, woodwork, and other subjects (Forster, 1982). Each family is issued with appropriate equipment to allow playback of the special media.

The schools encourage person-to-person contact, despite the distances between and remoteness of the students. A patrol program run by the Katherine School of the Air ensures that all students are visited twice a year for support purposes. Students also visit the school two or three times a year to chat with their teacher, and, where appropriate, do supplementary work (Forster, 1982). The schools also facilitate social events for the students. These include activity days, mini-schools, camps, and sports days, and allow students to meet (Mt Isa School of the Air, 1986). The camps allow supervisors to meet face-to-face, to discuss any issues which may have arisen (Forster, 1982). The school community sees the radio as just one tool that can be used for education and socializing.

The Port Augusta School of the Air used the radio medium in an innovative way to provide a student-centred learning experience (Rogers, 2000). Every Friday one of the students would run the thirty minute air lesson; the teacher took a back seat and effectively became another student. The technology allowed remote and distant students to learn about leadership and also about good peer-to-peer communication. When the peer session was science based, the student had to carefully explain the procedure step by step, thus enhancing their verbal communication skills. The student was also responsible for the preparation of the materials; the School of the Air then faxed the materials out to the other students.

The 1990s have seen the introduction of newer technologies in the Schools of the Air. This has improved the issues regarding lack of reliability in the communications systems (Rogers, personal communication, 2001). Examples of these technologies include computers with Internet connectivity, videoconferencing, and the "SkyConnect Tutor" system marketed by Telstra, Australia's major telecommunications company. Despite the improved reliability, 22% of respondents to a survey conducted by Boylan and Wallace (2000) felt that this new technology did not create an enhanced learning environment compared to that available through short-wave radio, although 95% of respondents to the same survey felt that the system enabled positive interactions between teacher and student. Some of this disquiet may have been due to difficulties, for example, finding support staff with the appropriate technical skills, and the cost of installation and maintenance of the equipment.

In both "Sesame Street" and the Schools of the Air, the technology was not seen as the focus of learning. In both cases, the technology was an adjunct to traditional learning methods, although "Sesame Street" assumed that the children would imitate and copy what was on the screen – no-one was necessarily present to check that they did so. In contrast, a feature of the Schools of the Air was the assumption that there would be a home tutor present during much of the learning.

The Role of ICT in the Lesson and Planning of the Lesson

The primary consideration when designing a lesson using ICT is how people learn, rather than what technology is available to the designer (Mayer, 2001). Technology is only another tool at the disposal of the educator, just like an overhead projector, textbook, or whiteboard, and the primary aim of any lesson should be to facilitate learning. Successful implementations of ICT in education cast the role of ICT as an adjunct to learning rather than the focus of learning (for example Chambers, 2001).

Integrating technology into the design phase of instruction leads to the full and appropriate use of technological resources (and their attributes) to best benefit the leaner. Considering the technology available also allows for the inclusion of novice/expert paradigms (for example Spiro et al, 1991; Van Lehn, 1989, p.565; Baddeley, 1982, p.39), which may be preferable for the relatively advanced learner. The use of novice/expert paradigms may go some way to assisting the teacher when planning for the different skill levels of their students. Presenting novice students with a representation of the expert's model may be more effective than allowing the novice learner to construct their own mental models (Kozma, 1994; Lai, 1989).

One commonly promoted feature of ICT is that it may be used in a self-contained manner, as evidenced by the proliferation of Computer Based Training packages which are marketed under taglines such as "Teach yourself Foo" and "Foo in 24 hours". Even packages which are seemingly well suited to the medium, such as typing tutors, cannot give the user guidance as how to correct their mistakes; they can simply advise the user that a mistake has been made. As with the use of short-wave radio, the presence of a human to provide higher-level cognitive feedback is important in correcting any problems the learner may have.

Physical access to the technology is another issue which needs to be considered when deciding on the role that ICT will play within a lesson. Typical considerations include: (1) will every member of the class need simultaneous access to the technology (a lab situation); (2) how disruptive is it (in the context of teaching a class) to get individual or groups of students to access the technology; (3) is sound an integral part of the technology (and what effect will that have on the rest of the room?); (4) what contingency plans are in place when the technology fails; (5) what impact will a technology failure have on the progress of the student; (6) what allowances have been made for access to the technology if the technology is going to be an integral part of assessment and submission; and (7) what mechanisms are in place to detect plagiarism.

Some of these decisions should be made during the lesson design and planning stage, rather than during the delivery of the lesson; others, such as the technology failure contingency plans and plagiarism detection, are issues that need to be worked through prior to the delivery, and actively monitored for the duration of the delivery and then implemented if and when necessary. The answers to these questions are all case-specific: they will vary from one educational setting to another. The important thing is that these questions are asked during the planning of the lesson or syllabus, answers found, and appropriate strategies set in place.

The contingency plan for technological failure is a consideration which is perhaps more applicable to ICT than any other technology previously used in an education context. If the use of the technology is limited to the presentation of a series of computer slides, then having the slides printed on transparencies and an overhead projector available in the same room is an adequate contingency. If the technology is going to be learner based, then questions which need to be addressed include: if the technology fails, is there enough time in the curriculum to reschedule the technology-based lesson (or a couple of weeks spare at the end of the term as a safety net for any slippages that may occur during the term); and if a catastrophe strikes (for example, a virus infects the computer system and renders it unusable for an extended period of time) then are there alternative delivery modes for lesson delivery and assessment submission available.

The more technology is integrated into the lesson, the more it becomes a single point of failure for the lesson, and the more work needs to be put into the development of a contingency plan. The level of contingency plan is a function of the way in which the technology was used. The Schools of the Air were conscious of unfavourable atmospheric conditions for radio transmission and reception; in this case, simply rescheduling the lesson to another time was suitable. In this case, the technology was being used as a delivery mechanism and is analogous to a presenter bringing along transparent overhead copies of their Powerpoint presentation. If the technology is going to be used to place the learner into a problem based learning environment through a simulation, say, then an appropriate contingency plan would be to have the same learning objectives as stated for the ICT-based simulation achieved via some other medium (for example a paper-based hypothetical which the learner can work through, a series of structured exercises, or a discussion forum).

Limitations and Capabilities of ICT

A guiding principle of software (and system) design is that, where possible, the designer must ensure that the technology meets the parameters of the system (Heckel, 1991). Designing a system around the limitations of the technology means that the system may not achieve what it sets out to do. The same is true for designing a syllabus or courseware which uses technology: the designer must be aware of the capabilities and limitations of the technology to be used, and ensure that the choice and use of technology does not compromise the pedagogical integrity of the course content. (Papert's Microworlds may seem to contradict this, in that the course was designed after the system was built, but in this case (and in many other areas where the technology is a focus of the syllabus), the limitations of the system are vital to the content)

It is important that the course designer be aware of the attributes of any tool they are going to use in a course. One of three things will happen when the designer considers the technology to be used in the course: (1) the attributes of the technology exceed those assumed in the course design; (2) the attributes are less than what has been assumed in the course design; (3) the attributes will almost perfectly complement the designed course. Commodity off the shelf (COTS) software and systems will generally fall into one of the first two categories, whilst the third category tends to only appear when the technology has been custom designed for the course.

One approach to using COTS software and systems in an educationally meaningful way is to spend some time evaluating the system, and then choose to use only those parts of the system which suit the learning objectives for the course. The educator then views ICT as just another resource at their disposal and freely picks and chooses which bits they want to use; just as they may only use one chapter from a textbook. This also allows the technology to fit the course design, rather than designing the course to fit the technology.

Custom-designing a system for a course is expensive, both in time and money, as is maintaining the content and the system, which can make this option unattractive. Custom built systems do have their advantages. They can be closely integrated into the course content, and can have examples and interfaces which are specifically designed for the educational purpose. Software has recently become available which is of sufficiently high usability and complexity (such as Macromedia Director) to allow the educator to concentrate purely on content development, without needing to worry about learning programming, or hiring a programmer. This has made custom-designed software and systems affordable, both in time and money, compared with five years ago, although the overheads for developing content in these systems is still far greater than for COTS. It is likely that these systems will become more common, and as they do, it is important that educators design the content and interface in a manner which complements learning.

Software and Multimedia Design

There have been several efforts at the compilation of the canonical list of aspects of good software/multimedia design. Heckel (1991) and Mayer (2001) are two examples of such lists. The near two decades between the compilation of these lists makes for a useful comparison in how thinking about how human interaction with computers has evolved. (Heckel's list was written in 1982; the second edition of his book (cited) does not alter the list, but provides more up-to-date examples).

Heckel (1991) proposes thirty rules to consider when designing computer software – his "Elements of Friendly Software Design". When Heckel's list was written Graphic User Interfaces were still to only be found in research laboratories and were at least two years away from being on user desktops. Heckel also included some elements which can be recognized as having a sound cognitive basis: making the user an active participant (Element 19, "Involve the User"); mental models (Element 13, "Support the Problem-Solving Process"); and differences in prior learning (Element 24, "Serve Both the Novice and the Experienced User"). Some software products now use the idea of progressive disclosure (Marchionini, 1991) through the use of "short menus", or a range of user modes, from "Beginner" through to "Expert".

Mayer (2001) proposes seven principles of multimedia design. They are: (1) Multimedia Principle: students learn better from words and pictures than from words alone; (2) Spatial Contiguity Principle: students learn better when corresponding words and pictures are presented near rather than far from each other on the page or screen; (3) Temporal Contiguity Principle: students learn better when corresponding words and pictures are presented simultaneously rather than successively; (4) Coherence Principle: students learn better when extraneous words, pictures and sounds, are excluded rather than included; (5) Modality principle. Students learn better from animation and narration rather than animation and on screen text; (6) Redundancy Principle: Students learn better from animation and narration than animation, narration and on-screen text; and (7) Individual Differences Principle: design effects are stronger for low-knowledge learners than for high-knowledge learners and for high spatial learners rather than for low-spatial learners.

Mayer has limited himself to pictures and words (including spoken word) only when considering multimedia. The focus of Mayer's research is qualitative rather than quantitative: what is learned, rather than how much is learned. A consequence of this approach is that Mayer's research places more emphasis on knowledge transfer than information retention.

Mayer also avers that "it is not productive to continue with traditional media research, in which one medium is compared to another." (p. 70). He has empirically tested the seven proposed principles, and found that the first six principles seem to hold true.

The Multimedia Principle assumes that the dual-channel information processing theory is valid. This theory states that there are two distinct and discrete input modes that learners use: a verbal mode, and a visual mode. Mayer demonstrates through example and empirical research that presenting new information as a combination of words and pictures (or animation and narration) assists in learner understanding more than the individual elements separately presented.

The Spatial Contiguity Principle argues that pictures and related text should be placed close to each other on the screen. This approach is superior to having the text and words separated for two reasons: first, it allows the learner to make associations between the text and pictures, thereby constructing links within their knowledge base; second, it reduces cognitive overhead by eliminating cross references (for example, "See Figure 5.1 on page 127") which require additional cognitive processing, and introduce the possibility of the learner looking at the wrong figure. The "Oscar Blending" segment from "Sesame Street", described earlier, is a good example of the Spatial Contiguity Principle in action.

The Temporal Contiguity Principle is effectively the same as the Spatial Contiguity Principle, with the time dimension the examined variable. As with spatial contiguity, Mayer argues that the simultaneous presentation of words and pictures leads to more effective learning, and concludes that "separating corresponding words and pictures in time detracts from multimedia learning." (p. 111). There was only a significant effect on learning when considering the transfer of knowledge; the study found that temporal dislocation of words and pictures had an insignificant effect on information retention.

The Coherence Principle states that students learn better when the information is concisely presented. Less extraneous information (noise) means that there are additional cognitive resources available for processing the useful information. The producers of Sesame Street empirically discovered the same principle in the early days of the show. The coherence principle can be used in reverse for assessment purposes: an educator wanting to use technology for problem based learning may add noise to the information to test the skills of the student in discriminating useful information.

The Modality Principle says that students learn better from animation and narration rather than animation and on screen text. This spreads the cognitive workload over two channels, resulting in less information coming through each channel, and therefore, under the dual-channel theory, makes learning more effective. Mayer's studies found that both retention and transfer were significantly improved when the modality principle was applied to a multimedia presentation. (Mayer's reference to modality refers to different modes of presenting information, and should not be confused with the Human-Computer Interface definition of modality).

The Redundancy Principle says that animation and narration lead to a better learning outcome than animation, narration, and on-screen text. These last three principles are all variations on a theme: overloading an input channel (in this case, the visual channel) has a negative effect on quality of learning.

It can be seen that the nature of the list content has changed over time; Heckel's list is comprised of broad guidelines, whilst Mayer's list focuses on a relatively fine-grained level of detail. Mayer has the advantage of assuming a

Graphic User Interface as standard; nonetheless, his list contents demonstrate both a technical advancement from Heckel's list, and a higher level consideration of cognitive principles when using technology for educational purposes.

Mayer also notes that verbal material presented in the first and second person is more effective than material presented in the third person. This is consistent with the success of inclusiveness in both short wave radio and "Sesame Street". Mayer's interpretation is that students work harder to understand when they feel as though they are actively involved in the learning experience.

Gredler (1986) notes that the use of computers for learning is largely restricted to drill-and-practice. In some simulations, which are members of the "variable assignment" class of simulations (Gredler, 1986), neither the basic problem nor the decisions required to solve it change once the correct solution has been determined. When designing exercises for multimedia based learning software, it is desirable that some form of knowledge transfer into a novel context occurs. This should demonstrate that learners are familiar with the concepts underlying the problem, rather than simply applying an algorithm which has been rote learnt. Once a learner has constructed knowledge, learners should be able to generalize it, hence transfer it into a novel context (Ullmer, 1992).

Common problems with the design of course and instruction which use ICT include:

- failing to consider technology from early in the design phase
- failing to account for the gradual shift in expertise by the participants during the course
- presenting the course participants with examples which fail to examine their transferability and generality of skills and knowledge. Such exercises only reapply rote algorithms to a particular problem; and do not verify that the concepts behind the solution are understood.

CONCLUSION

Information and Communications Technology can be used to increase the effectiveness of learning outcomes in both formal and informal educational settings. However, many of the lessons from the past that have been learnt by the pioneers of earlier technologies can still be adopted for use in today's learning environment. In particular, there are elements from the good use of television and radio which can apply to and directly inform ICT.

"Sesame Street" used a number of devices to ensure that effective learning took place in spite of the passivity of the television. These were:

- The producers had clearly defined learning outcomes;
- The programme was colourful without adding distracting information (noise);
- The programme used cinematic effects to recapture and maintain the viewers' attention;
- Ongoing testing of segments was performed, and unsuccessful segments removed or altered, and analyzed;
- The programme presented the viewer with a consistent interface;
- The producers hoped for imitation and practice from the viewers;
- The repetition of segments to reinforce ideas;
- The variation of the pace of the presentation to maintain viewer interest;
- The producers actively involved the viewer, through both the use of first and second person, and by encouraging practice and
- The producers did not assume that the TV show was going to be the sole source of learning for the viewer.

One result, applicable to ICT use today, was that when there was excessive (multimedia) activity going on, the children began to lose interest in the content (Gladwell, 2000).

An underlying philosophy of the Schools of the Air was that the technology was an adjunct to primary learning. The educational design of the Schools of the Air stressed the importance of human interaction with the learner. The teachers of the Schools of the Air also cleverly used the attributes of the medium to give students experiences and ask of them skills which would not have occurred in a traditional classroom.

In both of the cases of "Sesame Street" and the Schools of the Air, the respective attributes of television and radio were determined and then integrated into the educational design. It is important that the educator and course designer remember and apply cognitive principles when designing and implementing any course and consideration of Heckel's (1991) and Mayer's (2001) guidelines for good multimedia and software design should lead to a superior product for ICT in terms of usability and learning outcomes.

Ultimately, it is the responsibility of the educator to achieve the best learning outcomes possible for the students. The technology which best suits the learning outcome is the technology which should be used.

ACKNOWLEDGEMENTS

I would like to thank Dr Geoff Rogers of Charles Sturt University, NSW, Australia for his comments and suggestions on the Schools of the Air. Without his input, the section on the Schools of the Air would have been quite sparse.

Stephen Young, of the University of Melbourne, Australia, loaned me the book by Cliff Stoll, and discussed the book, which in turn started this chapter.

Finally, thanks to Cathi Colla for her love, support and encouragement, and general suggestions during the writing of this chapter.

REFERENCES

Atkins, M.J. (1993) Evaluating Interactive Technologies for Learning. *Journal of Curriculum Studies, 25(4),* pp 333-342.

Baddeley, A. (1982) *Your Memory: A User's Guide.* London: Penguin Books.

Baddeley, A. (1990) *Human Memory Theory and Practice.* Hove, UK: Lawrence Erlbaum Associates Ltd.

Boylan & Wallace (2000*) An analysis of classroom interaction patterns in satellite delivered lessons.* Paper presented at SPERA (Society for the Provision of Education in Rural Australia) Conference, 2000. Cairns, July 2000.

Brown, G. & Atkins, M. (1988) *Effective Teaching in Higher Education.* London: Methuen & Co Ltd.

Chambers, D.P. (2001) *Problem Based & IT Learning to Support Authentic Tasks in Teacher Education.* Proceedings of the 18th Annual Conference of the Australasian Society for Computers in Tertiary Education (ASCILITE). Melbourne, December, 2001.

Clarke, A.C (1993) Keynote speech at "Reinventing Schools: The Technology is Now". May 1993. The movie of the speech can be viewed at: http://search.nap.edu/html/techgap/media/aclarke/aclarke.mov

Cocking, R.R. & Mestre, J.F. (1989) *Cognitive Science.* (ERIC Document Reproduction Service No. ED 307 104).

Cognition and Technology Group (1991) Technology and the Design of Generative Learning Environments. *Educational Technology XXXI(5),* pp 34-39.

Collins, A. & Stevens, A.L. (1982) Goals and Strategies of Inquiry Teachers. In R. Glaser (Ed.) *Advances in Instructional Psychology Volume 2.* New Jersey: Lawrence Erlbaum Associates.

Daws, L. (1999) Dirt Roads, Bank Closures and Ice-Cream Cake for Little Lunch: Rural Communities and Education. In Meadmore, D, Burnett, B, and O'Brien, P (Eds) *Understanding Education: Contexts and Agendas for the new Millennium.* Sydney: Prentice Hall.

Eisenhart, M., Borko, H., Underhill, R., Brown, C., Jones, D., & Agard P. (1993) Conceptual Knowledge Falls Through the Cracks. *Journal for Research in Mathematics Education 24(1),* pp8-41.

Ellis, D., Ford, N., & Wood, F. (1993) Hypertext and learning styles. *The Electronic Library 11(1),* pp13-18.

Fisch, S. & Truglio, R. (2001) Why Children Learn from "Sesame Street". In Fisch, S. & Truglio, R (Eds.) *"'G' is for Growing: Thirty Years of Research on Children and Sesame Street".* Mahwah, New Jersey: Lawrence Erlbaum Associates, pp233-244.

Forster, MF (1982) Katherine School of the Air: The Bush School with a Difference. *Developing Education 9(3),* pp26-27.

Gagné, R.M., Briggs, L.J. & Wager, W.W. (1992) *Principles of Instructional Design.* Orlando, Florida: Holt Reinhart & Winston Inc.

Gardner, H. (1993) *Frames of Mind: The Theory of Multiple Intelligences (Tenth Anniversary Edition).* New York: BasicBooks.

Gladwell, M (2000) *The Tipping Point: How Little Things Can Make a Big Difference.* Boston: Little, Brown and Company.

Gredler, M.B. (1986) A Taxonomy of Computer Simulations. *Educational Technology XXVI(4),* pp7-12

Grider, C. (1993) *Foundations of Cognitive Theory: A Concise Review.* (ERIC Document Reproduction Service No. ED 372 324).

Haag, B.B. & Grabowski, B.L. (1995) The Design of CD-I: Incorporating Instructional Design Principles. *Educational Technology XXXV(2),* pp36-39.

Heckel, P. (1991) *(2nd Edition) The Elements of Friendly Software Design* San Francisco: Sybex.

Heckman, R.T. (1993) *Cognitive Science, Learning Theory and Technical Education.* Paper presented at the Annual International Conference of the National Institute for Staff and Organizational Development on Teaching Excellence and Conference of Administrators (15th, Austin, May 23-29, 1993) (ERIC Document Reproduction Service No. ED 361 049).

Kaplan, D (1986) *Television and the Classroom.* White Plains, New York: Knowledge Industry Publications, Inc.

Kozma, R.B. (1991) Learning with Media. *Review of Educational Research 61(2),* pp179-211.

Kozma, R.B. (1994) Will Media Influence Learning? Reframing the Debate. *Educational Technology, Research and Development 42(2)*, pp7-19.

Lai, K-W. (1989) *Acquiring Expertise and Cognitive Skills in the Process of Constructing an Expert System: A Preliminary Study.* (ERIC Document Reproduction Service No. ED 312 986).

Laurel, B. (1990) *The Art of Human-Computer Interface Design.* Reading, Massachusetts: Addison-Wesley Publishing Company.

Lesser, G (1974) Children and Television: Lessons from Sesame Street. New York: Random House.

Lesser, G. & Schneider, J (2000) Creation and Evolution of the "Sesame Street" Curriculum. In Fisch, S. & Truglio, R (Eds*.) "'G' is for Growing: Thirty Years of Research on Children and Sesame Street".* Mahwah, New Jersey: Lawrence Erlbaum Associates pp25-38.

Magidson, S. (1992) *From the laboratory to the classroom: A technology-Intensive Curriculum for Functions and Graphs.* Paper presented at the Annual Meeting of the American Educational Research Association (San Francisco, April 20-24, 1992) (ERIC Document Reproduction Service No. ED 352 017).

Marchionini, G. (1991) Psychological Dimensions of User-Computer Interfaces. ERIC Clearinghouse on Information Resources, Syracuse University, New York 13244-2340. (ERIC Document Reproduction Service No. ED 337 203).

Mayer, R (2001) *Multimedia Learning.* Cambridge: Cambridge University Press.

Miller, G.A. (1956) The magical number seven, plus or minus two: Some limits on our capacity for processing information. *Psychological Review* 63, pp81-97.

Mt. Isa School of the Air (1986) Kids Attend School by Satellite. *Curriculum Development in Australian Schools*, 2 June 1986, pp23-26.

Newell, A., Rosenbloom, P.S. & Laird, J.S. (1989) Symbolic Architectures for Cognition. In M. I. Posner (Ed.) *Foundations of Cognitive Science.* Massachusetts: MIT Press 93-132.

Palmer, E, & Fisch, S. (2001) The Beginnings of "Sesame Street" Research. In Fisch, S. & Truglio, R (Eds*.) "'G' is for Growing: Thirty Years of Research on Children and Sesame Street".* Mahwah, New Jersey: Lawrence Erlbaum Associates 3-24.

Reigeluth, C.M. & Schwartz, E. (1989) An instructional theory for the design of computer-based simulations. *Journal of Computer Based Instruction* 16(1). pp1-10.

Revelle, G., Medoff, L., & Strommen, E. (2001) Interactive Technologies Research at Children's Television Workshop. In Fisch, S. & Truglio, R (Eds.) *"'G' is for Growing: Thirty Years of Research on Children and Sesame Street"*. Mahwah, New Jersey: Lawrence Erlbaum Associates 215-230.

Riding R. & Buckle C. (1987) Computer Developments and Educational Psychology, Educational Psychology 7(1), pp5-11.

Rogers, G. (2000) Remote and isolated Children Learning Science. *In Investigating Australian Primary and Junior Science Journal,* ASTA 16(1), pp16-19.

Simon, H.A., & Kaplan, C.A. (1989) Foundations of Cognitive Science. In M. I. Posner (Ed.) *Foundations of Cognitive Science.* Massachusetts: MIT Press pp1-48.

Spiro R., Feltovich P., Jacobson M. & Coulson R. (1991) Cognitive Flexibility, Constructivism and Hypertext: Random Access Instruction for Advanced Knowledge Acquisition in Ill-Structured Domains. *Educational Technology* XXXI(5) pp24-33.

Sternberg, R.J. (1985) *Beyond IQ.* Cambridge: Cambridge University Press.

Stoll, C. (1999) *High Tech Heretic: Reflections of a Computer Contrarian.* New York: Anchor Books.

Thurman, R. & Mattoon, J. (1992) *Building Microcomputer-Based Instructional Simulations: Psychological Implications and Practical Guidelines.* Proceedings of Selected Research and Development Presentations at the Convention of the Association for Educational Communications and Technology and Sponsored by the Research and Theory Division. (ERIC Document Reproduction Service No. ED 348 034).

Ullmer, E.J. (1992) *Learning Environments: The Technology-Cognition Connection.* In Proceeding of Selected Research and Development Presentations at the Convention of the Association for Educational Communications and Technology and Sponsored by the Research and Theory Division. (ERIC Document Reproduction Service No. ED 348 035).

van Lehn, K. (1989) Problem Solving and Cognitive Skill Acquisition. In M. I. Posner (Ed.) *Foundations of Cognitive Science.* Massachusetts: MIT Press pp527-580.

Winn, B. (1988) *The Theoretical Foundations of Educational Technology and Future Directions for the Field.* Proceedings of Selected Research Papers presented at the Annual Meeting of the Association for Educational Communications and Technology (New Orleans, January 14-19, 1988).

SIMULATION: THE VISIBLE AND THE INVISIBLE

John Murnane

The use of computers for simulation and modeling dates back to the very earliest days of automatic calculation, and in particular to Whirlwind, the first computer ever designed to interact directly with a human (Redmond & Smith, 1980; vii). Whirlwind first ran in 1950–51 when it was used to train air defense operators. Fifty years later, simulation, modeling and direct machine-human interaction have become increasingly important to education. Harper, Squires and McDougall (2000) note that games and simulations have a long history of extensive and successful use in Australia. Feurzeig (1993) considers that computer modeling is an educational catalyst and provides a powerful new paradigm, bridging experiment and theory.

Teaching with computerised simulations, although powerful, is not entirely straight-forward. As with the use of any model there are simplifications and qualifications involved, and these may or may not be significant. There is also the question of the learning taking place: how well does the student's conception of the real world, as gained from the model, actually match reality?

PASSION AND UNDERSTANDING

The computer screen is an active filter. Much of what occurs in the face-to-face classroom is lost when material is directed through a computer: tonal inflections, expressions, the arm waving, some of the major clues a teacher uses to transmit their feelings for a subject. On the other hand it can add things the teacher cannot. It can provide the less tangible but invaluable benefit of giving its full attention to the student at all times, participating in a two-way information flow, remembering and processing various ideas. These qualities are put to good use in using a computer to run a simulation. Computer education pioneers such as Dwyer (1974) and Bitzer (1976) argued along these lines. Latterly computerised simulations have been associated with terms such as 'Constructivism,' 'active learning,' 'authentic environments' and 'situated learning.' (See Harper, Hedburg & Wright, 2000 and Harper, Squires & McDougall, 2000). On the other hand, Silverman (1993; pxii) remarked that his physics lecturers hardly showed any passion for the subject, either its theory or its apparatus The use of computerised models and simulations poses a challenge to teachers to maximize their own impact while simultaneously making best use of the things the computer can add.

Passion for a subject can be manifested in many ways but an essential ingredient is a desire on the part of the teacher to foster, in their students, a basic understanding for the material, something that demands more than simple regurgitation. As Silverman (1993; pxii) states, "And so conventional science instruction tells its beneficiaries what precisely they have to know, when they must know it, and how they must demonstrate on tests, homework and lab-work that they really know what they are supposed to."

The linked demands for teachers to engender understanding and interest in their students has important ramifications for using a computer for simulation for here, particularly, there is a requirement to consider all the factors involved, not just the reality to be modeled. One of the major factors is the simulation program itself. What appears on the screen, through the active filter, is only an end product. The totality of the system that produces the text and the graphics and the rest is at least of equal significance.

In some circles it's almost the fashion to downplay the computer—to ignore it as a thing. "You don't have to know anything about a computer to use one" I've heard said, offhand and sterile. If nothing else, it certainly lacks any trace of passion! Worse, 'You don't need to know anything about a computer to use one' is untenable as an educational idea. It assumes that a computer, including its programming, does not contribute to understanding. In fact, in any sort of educational context, any sentence beginning with 'You don't need to know...' is dangerous since it is only by understanding what is happening that students can pursue their own ideas and interests. Otherwise, almost by definition, they are only repeating the things the teacher (or program writer) included. Richard Feynman (1985; 36, 211), a motivational lecturer if ever there was one, writing about students who memorized their work, observed "their knowledge was so fragile." If he asked a question in any but the terms in which they had memorized they had no answer. And no way to find one. One of the reasons the computer can transform the classroom is that it gives teachers and students tools to deal with a wide variety of media—graphics, pictures, text, video, sound, speech and music. They can capture and create their own raw material, edit it and expose it to an audience using widely available and affordable tools. If students and teachers can use a word processor they have the skills to crop, move, assemble and title video clips. A modern basic digital video camera will outperform a very expensive and cumbersome analogue recorder. A digital editing suite costs about the same as a copy of MicroWorlds or ToolBook or comes free with the computer. Thus it provides the teacher with a powerful environment in which students can assemble a wide range of their own material. They are not just learning what they were told to learn. (See, Dwyer, 1971, 1974; Schnackenberg & Sullivan, 2000; Ping, 2001.)

This idea of teachers and students taking over the computer for their own ends predates the advent of the personal computer. Thomas Dwyer was Professor of Computer Science at the University of Pittsburgh when in 1971 he wrote a paper entitled "Some Principles for the Human Use of Computers in Education." In it he described what he referred to as a "new humanistic" view of education which encompasses the importance of utilising, paraphrased: 'the inherent curiosity of the human, the futility of imposing subject content on a student who does not perceive its acquisition as a rewarding experience and the unlimited potential of learners who elect to make the pursuit of some educational goal their own private crusade.' He proposed a marriage of this view with that of a technologist who suggests that 'extensive use of advanced technology can be used to shore up (or possibly replace) traditional school structures.' (Dwyer, 1971; 87.)

Dwyer drew an analogy with the dual/solo-mode sequence in flight instruction. "This is a learning situation which develops advanced cognitive and motor skills for students of quite varied backgrounds, and which also involves many affective elements, but which relies heavily on technology for achieving these ends. While it is clear that dual instruction is essential (one does not recommend that a student immediately go out in an aeroplane and 'do his own thing') it is equally clear that the student will optimise his benefits from the dual mode if he knows he is preparing for a solo flight. He knows, in fact, that he can eventually exert more influence on his learning than his instructor....computer technology in education should invite similar control at all levels. It should, in particular, invite the student to 'go behind the scenes' (possibly acting in concert with teachers) at any time they elect. There should be no secrets, or one-upmanship of the adult world over the student world." (Dwyer, 1971; 233)

If nothing else this demonstrates the idea that it is not necessary to continually modify educational philosophy simply because some of the tools involved happen to be constantly gaining in power and flexibility. This brings us directly to reality, and to modeling.

REALITY AND MODELING

The Technical University of Munich website contains the following description: "Simulation is copying a system with its dynamic processes in a experimental model, in order to arrive at realizations, [that] are portable to the reality." (Reinhart, 2001.) These interpretations will be of use in the following sections.

Simulation is arguably one of the most powerful ways in which a computer can be used in a classroom, but without for a second wishing to downplay the possible scope of this contribution it does have limitations and these limitations should be examined along with its promise. The more powerful a teaching method is, the more damage it will do if it is used inappropriately.

There are some potentially problematic aspects to computerised models which do need to be always kept in the foreground of teachers' minds but which are sometimes overlooked. By and large these factors are not simply negatives, they are an inherent part of the discipline. Rarely are these factors addressed in documentation accompanying educational software, perhaps because they are seen as universals. They require delineation so that they become part of the educational decisions on which simulations to employ, in what conditions, and how they are to be used. Reducing these factors to their bare bones leads to a question: 'the model, or the message?'

The Model

A model is something which is manipulated to explore the dynamic behavior of some part of the real world. Usually it is the behaviour of a system which is of interest. It might involve a fairly simple artifact, like a car or a camera, something larger on the scale of a Saturn moon rocket, or something with the complexity of the entire hardware system and its control which took us to the moon, or on the same scale, a smallish ecosystem.

In terms of commercial products used in Australian classrooms this covers programs such as "Hot Dog Stand," "James Discovers Maths," "Maths Circus," "Gears," "Widget Workshop," "Exploring the Nardoo" and the "Biology Explorer" series, all of which contain simulations of various types. There is an immediate question: exactly which parts of the areas suggested by these titles are actually modeled?

The Message

The 'behaviour' of a system can cover a lot of territory. There is what is usually called the 'black box' approach. The user does not know what is happening inside it, but is interested in what it does. In terms of the classroom, this might be called the 'message.' You do *this*, and it does *that*.

Black box testing is concerned with only two things: inputs and outputs. The experimenter tries a range of inputs and observes the results. Sometimes the set of inputs will be limited as will be their range. In "Exploring the Nardoo" (Brickell, 1998), a user can alter a set of parameters which govern the health of an imaginary but typical Australian river system. Sliders control the amount of sunlight, river flow, agricultural run-off etc. The model then reports on the subsequent behaviour of several output parameters. Because of the set ranges provided by the sliders, students can fairly easily explore the entire range for all settings.

In a program such as SimCity (1998) which is used in Sociology in some Australian and American schools (Teague & Teague, 1995; Kolson, 1994), the possible variations are essentially endless. The limits of the system are not defined and the range of various settings are not inherent in the interface. For instance the size of the created city is only limited by the size of the map, that is, the size of the playing area, and the time spent playing. Essentially, the longer you play, the bigger it gets. If you wish to situate a nuclear power plant in the centre of your metropolis you can. It's a good place for it from many practical considerations such as ease of power distribution. In contrast, a simulation written specifically to teach about nuclear power may well behave rather differently!

It is quite likely that the SimCity type of open ended situation not only applies to a greater part of the real world than the more closed examples, but they are also likely to be more interesting. They require more from the teacher in terms of determining the student's readiness to use the model, guidance in manipulating it and in evaluating how far the student has progressed towards determining the overall behaviour of the system. For instance, clues to the student's understanding might be given by:

- Have they deduced any relationships between the input and output parameters? Is it a quantifiable relationship or just a general association of some sort? If they can see a direct relationship is it linear?
- Do any range of settings of various parameters form an equivalence class? That is, for any parameter or parameters, are there any ranges of setting whose effect can be considered together or considered to be equivalent?
- Are there any 'break points' where a small change can produce a disproportionate effect? For instance, in investigating dam levels in Exploring the Nardoo, (Brickell, 1998), regardless of the slider setting, 'Permanent Irrigation' has small effects right across the 10 year simulated cycle, but 'Annual Irrigation' shows a distinctly asymptotic effect. Between months 51 and 52, at a setting of 12 on a 0–15 scale, dam levels go from full to empty and do not recover.

Black box modeling has a lot in common with the operant conditioning school of psychology developed in the 1950's by B. F. Skinner (1953,1963). It considers the observable 'response' of 'the organism' to a 'stimulus' and nothing else. The experimenter provides the stimulus and observes the (physical) result. This is a very scientific and repeatable process and an understanding of its associated learning theory can be a useful tool in education. It lead directly to Programmed Learning and the 'teaching machine' (Skinner, 1963). However since it ignores all 'internal states' of the learner it is necessary to understand that this type of approach, either to students or to models, is limited.

In general a black box exploration of a model should take place before any information is made available about its workings. Models are meant to effect an exploration of the real world and this exploration should take place before any analysis of its actual functions. This is in line with modern Constructivist learning theory. (See Harper, Squires & McDougall, 2000) Treating a model as a black box allows the user to determine at least some of its designed operating functions. For a simple model it may determine them all. For more sophisticated models time constraints or complexity induced by interaction between parameters may not allow the full range of responses to be explored. Harper, Squires & McDougall (2000) note that complexity may provide authentic learning environments, but could make learners insecure and lose track of learning objectives.

Exploration, experimentation and, subsequently, hypothesis testing is the very essence of simulation. However, just as Operant Conditioning ignores anything but overt, observable behaviour, treating a model as a black box ignores any information that its internal workings ('states') can provide. This information may range from trivial to vital.

A good example can be seen in 'Lunar Lander,' an early computerised simulation requiring the user to input a set of correct 'throttle openings' which would cause the 'lander' to touch down safely on the moon. I vividly remember spending hours trying to discover a set of values which would successfully land the thing. Despite being eventually told that my landing was 'as gentle as a kitten's purr' I actually learnt absolutely nothing about either the physics or the dynamics of the process. My values were all completely empirical and determined largely by a need to use a set pattern (based on doubling then halving the throttle openings), so that I could easily remember them!

I wish to argue that both teachers and students should be able to look at the workings of a simulation, otherwise they are, like Skinnerian psychologists, deliberately ignoring potentially valuable information. Certainly the teacher may wish to control the point at which the student can look inside the model but the possibility of doing so should exist. If a model captures any of whatever aspect of reality it purports to represent, then looking at how it does that should provide clues to the way reality functions. Its simplifications and limitations should also be available. This is not usually possible with commercial computerised simulations.

This is not to suggest that access to the program itself is required. Certainly in a commercial product that probably would not be particularly helpful, and it is not in any way necessary. But the 'model' itself is a different matter, and that can be explained in any number of convenient ways. Assuming the model is being used in a valid educational context by a competent teacher it is reasonable to expect that the teacher understands the academic area and its principles. Hence they should be able to understand the workings of the model if these are available. It is not a question of whether black box model manipulation is better than a transparent approach, the only important question is 'When will looking at the workings help the learning process?' For any simulation sufficiently complex to be interesting this is likely to be when the student has gained a good understanding of the reactions of the model to a range of inputs and has made, or begun to make, good and verifiable observations about its subsequent behaviour.

Simulation

Simulating a dynamic system with a computer programme is one form of modeling. Since a model can be anything short of the real thing, 'model' spans a good deal of territory. Many people have constructed and flown a model aeroplane—whether it's just a paper dart or built from balsa. By just flying the paper dart the modeler learns about lift and drag and buffeting and stalling speed, even if they don't know them by those names.

A computerised simulation is a much more abstract form of model than the paper aeroplane. It may involve 'hardware' of some description, perhaps a 'force feedback' joy stick, but it is more concerned with a mathematical approach. It is the process of imitating a real system with a set of mathematical formulae or tables (Reinhart, 2001). Most teachers who have used computers will have seen, and more than likely used, simulations. A programmer builds a model of the real thing and the user can then manipulate it. However while some of these, for instance Microsoft's Flight Simulator, (Microsoft, 1997) implement the model using precisely defined and rigorously tested mathematical formulae, others use far less precise approximations. Unless the accompanying documentation describes the way a particular simulation is implemented there may be no way to decide which is the case. One of the inherent attributes of the computer is that unlike a paper aeroplane you can't see what it is doing or how it is doing it.

Simulations may be imprecise because of the complexity of the reality they model. Every ecosystem will contain things biologists do not know about or only understand imprecisely. Equally there are some things the modeler might know, but which contain more complexity than they want to expose to the students or can comfortably contain within the scope of the program. Edward (1996) makes a particular point of this in describing a simulation used in training offshore oil workers. "In particular students were expected to appreciate the deficiencies of the model in predicting reality." This type of observation is not common in the literature (although see Kolson,1994), and even rarer, if not actually non-existent, in commercial products. Assuming a useable model, the key word is 'manipulate.' The essence of a simulation is human intervention. Humans playing 'what if'? Humans deciding, within the rules of the game, what are the inputs and the parameters, and then looking at the changing outputs: the model's behaviour.

Simulations allow experimentation with a slice of the real world in a play situation. By playing with the model you learn how to use it. That is, *you learn about the model*. Since the model is not the reality you may or may not learn correctly about that section of the real world it simulates (See Edward, 1996; Magin & Reizes, 1990).

Two Mental Models

Given that, by definition, a simulation is not reality, the use of a simulation in the classroom involves the development of two separate mental models. There is the mental model related to the manipulation of the simulation, and the mental model linking the simulation to the real world. These models may be indistinguishably coincident or they may have almost no overlap. The degree to which the two do coincide is a measure of the educational success of the simulation.

The two different mental pictures should not be taken for granted, even where the link between the two is very close, as, say, in counting bottle tops to simulate counting apples. The differences must always be borne in mind. With computerised simulations, the simulated reality does not need to be very complex for this link to become obscure fairly quickly.

The relationship between the User and the model is largely the provenance of good interface design. There is something intuitive about a hammer. Look at one and you know how to pick it up and what it's good for. A good human-computer interface should exhibit not only the same high level of performance as a hammer, but also its strong and immediate sense of purpose.

A good interface designer can often build this sort of obvious functionality into their creations. But to be useful, the correct mental model must be developed and the relationship of the computerised model to the real world should be considered. Learning about a model may be interesting but the idea is to learn about that which it models. As an example the Apollo space program provides excellent material for anyone studying the educational use of modeling. Modeling and simulation were used extensively to design the parts of the system, then simulations were used to train the personnel. Situations arising during training frequently fed back into the system design itself (See Murray & Cox, 1989; 343).

Murray and Cox (1989; 328), writing about the difficulty of piloting a spacecraft into orbit around the moon, wrote: "Mayer could understand why it seemed tricky to a layman. It was comparable to taking a rifle outside his office in Building 30... and aiming it at a basketball in downtown Houston, some twenty-six miles away. Actually, it was even tougher than that, more like aiming at a point one-sixteenth of an inch to the side of the basketball. So, yes, Mayer could see why a layman might think it was tricky. Pavelka, who wasn't a layman, decided it was legitimate to be nervous. 'We just simulated the hell out of this stuff, but there was never proof that it all fit to together, you know?'"

The task of navigating a spacecraft to the moon is not something which can be solved precisely with a set of equations and is a classic example of the need for information derived from simulations. The model is used to predict the future: how the first Apollo spacecraft to orbit the moon might behave.

The Apollo simulations didn't always work well. NASA ran some preliminary analysis to see what the second stage of a Saturn would do if two of its five engines expired. The results were grim and they didn't bother with it any further. So when two adjacent engines, which was the worst case, shut down on the unmanned Apollo Six the controllers just reached for their abort buttons. But, "contrary to all predictions, the thing seemed to be flying." So they rode it out and managed to complete most of the test maneuvers in the flight plan and return the spacecraft safely to earth. The model had actually given them a misleading answer (Murray & Cox, 1989; 310.).

Simulations do not take into consideration all the factors in the real-world article: that's why they are models. (See Towne, 1995, Chapter 4). There are at least five main differences:

- Omissions: there may be aspects of reality the model omits.
- Simplifications: every model simplifies some or all aspects of the thing it models.
- Approximations: Mathematical formulae may only approximate the dynamics or Organisation of the real thing. In fact, they may not actually 'model' the behaviour at all—they might just form an empirical approximation.
- Physical analogies: a physical model will not possess all the characteristics of the real thing or may not be an accurate reflection of them.
- There may be things about the real thing the model cannot do at all: a person running Flight Simulator is not going to experience aircraft movement yet the pilot of an actual aeroplane will feel it and the pilot is part of the real world.

In one sense, it could be argued that Software Engineers have it easy, they are implementing systems which are ends in themselves. They are not attempting to teach about a system, just to provide control of one. They only have to address whether the mental model of the user matches the computer model? In learning from a simulation there is the extra step: from mental model to computerised model to physical reality. With an extra 'mapping' there is at least twice as much chance for error and probably much more.

In the simplest educational simulations, the relationship of the computerised model to reality is quite obvious. In one of the Maths Circus (Luckett, Mitchell, & Smith,1999) screens the student sorts objects into categories. There is also a 'counting model' where the User counts the objects and enters the number.

The next level of modeling, where the modeled phenomena are complex, is far more difficult. Here, the working of the computerised model may not be obvious, or even vaguely apparent, at all. So how is the teacher to determine what was learned?

How Does a Simulation Relate to a Reality?

To the people in the Apollo Mission Control Room the simulations never felt like games, or even practice runs. "Their verisimilitude, and the seriousness with which they were taken, reproduced even the emotions of the real thing." (Murray & Cox, 1989; 298.) That was vital, because practice under pressure was part and parcel of the training.

When program alarms sounded on the first descent to the moon, essentially the computer announcing it was totally overloaded and the controllers had seconds to decide whether to abort the landing, Jack Garman was sure he knew what was causing it. He'd been through uncounted simulations, including a 'program alarm' although that had only occurred once, and that more-or-less by accident! "...if it does not occur again, we're fine," he said, and they were (Murray & Cox, 1989; 352).

"For the next minute Garman listened as the crew performed the final maneuvers before landing. The adrenaline rush that swept him during the program alarms faded, leaving him drained, with a detached sense of watching the events in slow motion. It was then he heard Aldrin in Eagle say, 'Forty feet, down two and a half. Picking up some dust.' Garman was startled out of his trance. Everything had felt just like the simulations until then. But Aldrin had never said 'Picking up some dust.' The image of the dust blowing up around the LEM made it real, and the enormity of it began to sink in." (Murray & Cox, 1989; 352)

Just what is the overlap between real experience and a simulation? Are the two things disjointed? Are they virtually the same? Does the student have a grasp of how the model works, and are they applying what they have learned of the model to the real world? For any simulation, the teacher needs to know the following:

- Has the student learned to predict what the simulation will do under different circumstances?
- Has the student decided anything about how the model works?
- Can the student apply knowledge gained from the simulation to the real world?
- How closely does the student's mental model now match the real world?

If any of these factors are unknown or indeterminate the teacher will not be able to satisfactorily judge the learning outcomes for the lesson. Nor will they be ιn a position to help fill gaps in the student's knowledge base, reinforce what is right, correct what is wrong and make links to other related material.

- If the student cannot make predictions about the model, the simulation is a failure. If the predictions are wrong the student may have an incorrect mental model of the simulation. The teacher can only hope they do not apply this to the real world.
- If the student does not have at least a reasonable idea about the way the simulation is functioning they will be in a very poor position to relate their experience to the real world. As Feynman (1985; 26) points out, without understanding, knowledge is so fragile. He goes further, (ibid.; 211), reflecting at some length on the complete inability of students who have 'learned' without understanding to apply their 'knowledge' to anything else, however closely related.
- If the student can deduce or apply things learnt from the model to the real world the use of the simulation is a success.
- Finally, the teacher would (at least ideally) like an exact picture of how the student now sees that part of the real world under study.

If a teacher elects to use a particular piece of software, it could be assumed that they should be sufficiently expert in their discipline to know what the model is doing. In many cases the answer is likely to be that they do not. Even the best Biology teacher is not going to know everything about a particular ecosystem. Manocchie (1999) remarks of SimCity that its "incorporation ...into sociology courses can provide both interactive and experiential learning," but it would be most unlikely that any teacher understood all the relevant factors and there is no information available in the program's documentation on how these are actually modeled. The manual will suggest strategies which can be used, for instance that building bus stations will help lower car traffic and pollution in their local area but it does not say how this is implemented. (SimCity, 1998.) Kolson (1994), while supporting its use in an urban planning class, details eight specific limitations of SimCity and three "insoluble problems." He notes that "most of the [problems] have already been addressed in SimCity 2000" but the insoluble problems, which he considers are major and fundamental to city planning, remain. Teague and Teague (1995), discussing the same program refer to only one of Kolson's 'problems,' that of its failure to allow for deficit budgeting. Given that there remain areas of disagreement among urban planners it is to be expected that problems with this class of program are endemic. (Kolson, 1994.)

For all but simple simulations, the teacher needs to know the following:

- Is there a description of the model?
- Are the simplifications listed?
- Are the approximations described?
- Are any limitations specified?
- What are the assumptions on which the simulation is based?

Lessons learned from the development of simulations can illustrate these points. The author of any simulation program may not be the author of its specifications. It is well established practice for software to be developed by a team rather than an individual. One part of the team can develop the specifications and equations and another implement the interface. Dwyer (1971) noticed that in helping a teacher develop a simulation on Pennsylvania Maple trees, starting from "zero" his knowledge of them had "zoomed upward to almost professional level." Previously, his knowledge of Maple tress was non existent, but in order to make a program work he had to study and comprehend the model. Just studying the model (and, presumably, progressively testing the emerging simulation), lead to a strong understanding of the reality.

There is plenty of scope for the use of simulations in educational practices. This scope would be enhanced if the simulation was more transparent.

REFERENCES

Bitzer, D. L. (1976). Plato, An adventure in learning. *Seventh Australian Computer Conference*. Perth: Advanced Press.

Brickell, G. [Ed.] (1998). *Exploring the Nardoo*. Classroom Edition. Belconnen, Australian Capital Territory: Interactive Media.

Dwyer, T. A. (1971). Principles for the human use of computers in education. *International Journal of Man-Machine Studies*, 3, pp219–239.

Dwyer, T. A. (1974). Heuristic strategies for using computers to enrich education. *International Journal of Man-Machine Studies*, 6. Reprinted in Taylor, R. P. (1980). *The Computer in the School: Tutor, Tool, Tuttee*. New York: Teachers College Press.

Edward, N. S. (1996). Evaluation of computer based laboratory simulation. *Computers & Education*, 26, pp123–130.

Feynman, R. (1985). *Surely you're joking Mr Feynman*. New York: Norton.

Feurzeig, W. (1993). Visualization in educational computer modeling. In Towne, D., de Jong, T. & Spada, H. [Eds.] (1993). *Simulation-Based Experiential Learning* Berlin: Springer-Verlag.

Harper, B., Hedburg, J. G. & Wright, R. (2000). Who benefits from virtuality? *Computers and Education,* 34, pp163–176.

Harper, B., Squires, D. & McDougall, A. (2000). Constructivist simulations: A new paradigm. *Journal of Educational Multimedia and Hypermedia,* 9(2), pp115–130.

Kolson, K (1994). The politics of city planning simulations. Paper presented at the *Annual Meeting of the American Political Science Association,* September 1–4.

Luckett, S., Mitchell, B. & Smith, D. (1999). *Maths Circus.* Rev. ed. Ashgrove, Qld.: Greygum Software.

Magin, D. & Reizes, J. (l990). Computer simulation on laboratory experiments: the unexplored potential. *Computers & Education,* 4, pp263–270.

Manocchie, M. (1999). SimCity 2000 software. *Teaching Sociology,* 27 (2), pp212.

Microsoft Flight Simulator 98. (1997). US: Microsoft.

Murray, C. & Cox, C. (1989). *Apollo: The Race to the Moon.* London: Secker & Warburg.

Ping, C. (2001) Learner control and task-orientation in a hypermedia learning environment. *International Journal of Instructional Media,* 28 (3), pp271–215.

Redmond, K. C. & Smith T. M. (1980). *Project Whirlwind.* Massachusetts: Digital Press.

Reinhart, I. G. (2001). Institute for Machine Tools and Industrial Management. Technical University of Munich. http://www.iwb.tum.de/projekte/sim_i_bay/definition:Dg.html.

Schnackenberg, J. & Sullivan, H. (2000). Learner control over full and lean computer-based instruction under differing ability levels. *Educational Technology, Research and Development,* 42(2), pp19–38.

Silverman, M. (1993). *And Yet It Moves: Strange Systems and Subtle Questions in Physics.* New York: University Press.

SimCity 3000 Unlimited. (1998). Redwood City, CA: Maxis.

Skinner, B. F. (1953). Some contributions of the experimental analysis of behavior to Psychology as a whole. *American Psychologist,* 8, pp 69–78.

Skinner, B. F. (1963). *Science and Human Behavior.* New York: Macmillan.

Teague, M. & Teague, G. (1995). Planning with computers–a social studies simulation. *Learning and Leading With Technology,* 23(1), pp20–22.

Towne, D. M. (1995). *Learning and Instruction in Simulation Environments.* Englewood Cliffs, New Jersey: Educational Technology Publications.

ZONES OF INTERPRETIVE DEVELOPMENT IN EDUCATION AND MULTIMEDIA DESIGN

Susan Rodrigues

INTRODUCTION

Constructivism is a school of thought that has influenced educational research for several decades. This school of thought has led to general agreement that individuals make sense of their experiences by making links to their existing knowledge. Many educators and designers believe they are creating multimedia courseware within and influenced by a Constructivist framework. On a basic level, Constructivism is governed by the notion that everyone is responsible for their personal negotiation of meaning based on previous experience. Vygotsky (1962) reported that children in cooperation with others performed at a higher cognitive level than children working in isolation. Due to the fact that Vygotsky viewed learning as a social process, he emphasised dialogue. In light of these ideas, tasks that are underpinned by Constructivist views tend to start from the learner's perspective, involve some form of cooperation and/or involve engagement in authentic tasks.

Not surprisingly, the potential of technology to provide users with opportunities to make links has been widely included in the rhetoric of most pro-technology users. As a direct consequence, current software is often marketed as constructivist, due mainly to the fact that access to information is non-linear and in some instances because computer based learning offers scope for personal or communal interaction. In the development of software, this type of open access is often considered a Constructivist trait, simply because the pathway taken by the user is user determined. The inclusion of Hyperlinks and autonomous access to a range of pathways has led some to suggest that instructional systems designers are influenced by Constructivist philosophy.

In contrast, designers influenced by Behaviourist views of learning (see for example, Gagne, 1970) propose that the correct sequencing of conceptual knowledge in tandem with a mastery approach can lead to learning. The design of early tutorial systems, which were predominantly drill and practice activities involving pre-sequenced material, are examples of Behaviourist influenced ICT. Behaviourist influenced designers lean towards the inclusion of fragmented key concepts that eventually, with the right teacher, form the bigger picture. A behaviourist-influenced designer would assess learning by quantifying the learning in some way.

Some of the strengths of behaviourist tutorials, for example, repeat practice, reinforcement and control, are not advocated by Constructivist philosophies (Heinich, 1984), where the notions of reflection, active construction, personal relevance and autonomy (Lebow, 1993) are considered crucial Constructivist learning facets. Behaviourist learning environments provide extrinsic goals and rewards, whereas, Constructivist approaches promote an intrinsic notion of success and metacognition.

Regardless of the developments in learning theory, in the 1980s there was speculation regarding the incompatibility of Constructivist assumptions and instructional design system methods. Reigeluth (1989) contended that ICT instructional systems and Constructivist philosophies required a positivist tradition to fuse with Constructivist views of learning. Dick (1991) suggested that the dilemma of seemingly incompatible and contradictory stances could be addressed in two ways. The multimedia theory base could be influenced by Constructivist ideology, or the multimedia could be employed as a tool in situated practice within a classroom underpinned by Constructivist ideology. In this chapter I will look more closely at the challenges I faced in trying to influence the multimedia theory base. I will explain why grounding multimedia design in constructivist philosophy is problematic.

One of the key reasons for the difficulty lies in the fact that grounding design in learning theory requires a negotiation and shared understanding of terms. Another reason for the difficulty lies in the fact that although the technology is evolving at a rate of knots, it is still limited in terms of the kind of scaffolding espoused and required by Constructivist theory. Progress in technological development may be providing opportunities to address some Constructivist ideals, but fundamental issues of metacognitive strategies and scaffolding are more difficult to incorporate. Already, in this chapter I have used words that have specific meanings for an educator. Words like 'scaffolding' and 'metacognition' have to be interpreted by the designer if we want successful translation of requirements into reality. The interpretive process is explored in this chapter with a view to documenting some of the challenges and opportunities faced by designers and educators. It builds on what Davidson-Wasser and Bresler (1997) consider interpretive zones. The process of collaborative work and the influence and expectation of group members' experience will have a significant impact on the development of a particular product. Vygotsky's notion of the Zone of Proximal Development, ZPD, (1962) refers to the zone in which learning occurs in the presence of scaffolding by a more informed other. In the development of educational software, there are more informed others with respect to learning theory and with respect to software development, so there is a need for reciprocal support. The informed other is expert in their own domain and novice in the other, so a software designer is an expert in the field of design and relatively inexperienced in the area of learning theory, while the educator is unlikely to be a design expert. These degrees of expertise have an impact on the multimedia design process.

Instructional multimedia design processes and approaches highlight the need to identify key objectives, pertinent strategies, and diagnostic evaluations. Yang, Moore, and Burton (1995) describe a three-stage instructional design model that proposed different activities and responsibilities for those involved in the design of courseware. Liu, Jones, and Hemstreet (1998) proposed six main phases for effective multimedia design projects: funding, planning, designing, producing, testing and marketing. This chapter tracks one particular design project, from its inception to its conclusion in order to illustrate how situating multimedia design within a constructivist framework is both challenging and opportunistic.

In this chapter I focus on four of Liu, Jones, and Hemstreet's (1998) proposed six main phases: the planing, designing, producing, and testing elements. Funding for the project was relatively easy, the University made available funds to track the development and the software designers saw this as an opportunity to create a product that would be used in schools. Marketing has also proved to be relatively easy as word of mouth resulted in people requesting copies of the CDROM.

FUSING HORIZONS: EDUCATION RESEARCH
AND SOFTWARE DESIGN

To a certain extent, some of the Constructivist ideals have been simply interpreted. For example, CDROMs are touted as Constructivist because they allow for user choice and access. One could however argue that, at that level, the user has the same degree of choice and access with a normal textbook. The user could browse through a book/CDROM, flit from page/screen to page/screen and decide on where they want to start and finish. As an educational researcher involved in researching the use of ICT in teaching and learning science, I was drawn to investigate how a CDROM on the topic of atomic structure and the periodic table, that took on board Constructivist ideas, could be created for students aged 14 –15 years. I had also been asked to propose a project for a computer software engineering course where final year honours student designers work with clients on realistic tasks. So, I became a 'client'. The final year students were keen to meet the requirements of the client and I was conversant with Constructivist ideas, so I thought this would be a good opportunity to see how effectively we could incorporate Constructivist ideas in the design of a CDROM for school aged pupils.

The team of four software designers were conscientious workers. They were determined to interpret and translate my requirements into reality. I also felt that I was well informed by research on cognition and Constructivist ideals. Therefore we had the best case scenario for the design and preparation of a CDROM that is influenced by Constructivist views.

I agreed to a software requirements specification and we then held meetings to discuss and translate expectation into reality. Soon the designers began to interpret the requirements to create a package (See Figure 1).

I worked with four software designers and I monitored the project by audiotaping and then transcribing meetings, collecting and analysing our email messages, and monitoring the work in progress through a web site managed by the software designers. The designers gave me access to minutes from designer-only meetings and provided hard copies of documentation related to the project.

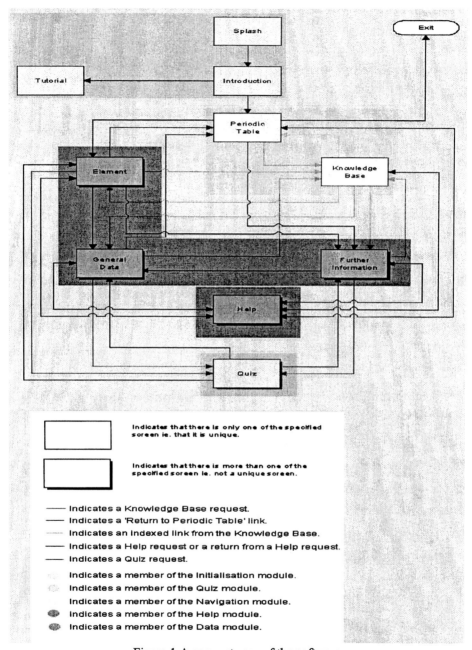

Figure 1 A concept map of the software

When the project commenced I asked the four software designers to complete and email me their responses to a questionnaire that sought to identify their views of teaching and learning. The emailed questionnaire asked open-ended questions such as:

- What do you think are the software requirements?
- What do you think are the strengths of the package you are developing?
- Why do you consider them strengths?
- What is the most difficult client demand to interpret?
- What is the easiest client demand to accomplish?

Additional questions were emailed to the designers whenever I wanted clarification of their views and when I wanted more information. To ensure some degree of validity I gave the transcripts and other data to the designers for perusal and comment and I have made an article documenting our interaction available to them.

Planning and Designing: The Role of Language

I thought the written software requirement specification was clear. But I made one key assumption. I assumed that the designers and I would interpret the written software requirement specification in the same way. Indeed it was clear from the outset that these designers intended to follow the specification:

> ...it is common practice to write a requirements document as the first phase of a software engineering cycle. It helps to ensure that the programmers and the client are speaking the same language. It ensures that the product is built to the client's specification and that everything the client wants will be designed and then implemented. (Desginer 2. 19S email communication)

The excerpt above suggests an assumption that the nomenclature used would be commonly interpreted by all present so that we would all be 'speaking the same language'. We used common words, but what soon became apparent was that our frames of reference for these words were different.

Take for example the word 'help'. A simple and useful word. A word that has serious implications for the user of software. The 'help' facility and advice statement were crucial facets because we wanted to minimise cognitive overload while promoting learner control of navigation. So, not surprisingly, 'help' is a crucial element of any software. The software designers and I met to discuss the content and context of some of the screens. Preliminary screens (see figure 2 for an example) were posted on the Internet for team perusal and comment. It was during one of these meetings to discuss the content and context of the screens that we realised we were using the same language to talk about different things. The 'help' facet was discussed during an early meeting and the following transcript, taken from this meeting, shows how we managed a conversation assuming that we were interpreting the words in the same way, when the reality was quite different.

I have selected an excerpt that shows the start of our thinking about other screens, having just concluded a discussion about screens for the first twenty elements (See figure 2).

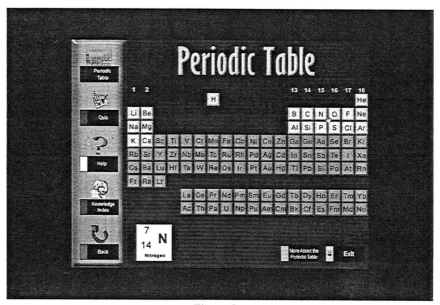

Figure 2

We were, until this point, working under the assumption that we shared meaning for the word and concept of 'help' as used in the software requirement specification. In the transcripts, R refers to me and I have used, 1, 2, 3 and 4 to represent the designers. If there was an interruption, I have used '-' and I have used '...' to represent editing for ease of reading.

Figure 3 An example of the help screen for magnesium.

I saw the inclusion of 'help' as a scaffolding device: a way of helping the students understand the concept. The designers perceived 'help' as the necessary tool to help students navigate through the CDROM. We maintained a conversation, using the word 'help' with significantly different interpretations. It was well into the conversation when we realised this, and even then it was a fluke and arose because one of the designers wanted confirmation of the screen template (see figure 3).

Verbatim transcript

R What about then, if I go to this one near the, go to the help button on lithium. Here. What's it going to take me to?

3 It's going to be a screen almost identical to the other help screen, like it's going to say you wanted help with lithium.

1 Yeah but what's going to be on that page though....

R Is it going to be about atomic mass or is it going to be about-

2 -No! It'll be about using that screen.

3 Using that particular screen.

R This isn't about using this help screen, isn't about using the screen it's about context.

4	No, no.
3	Hang on. I'll give you, give you an example OK? You've got your lithium screen. Now what this bit here will contain is a shrunken version of the actual screen, which you just came from. As an example. With arrows and little arrows and diagrams saying press this button to do this.
R	Oh, right.
3	Press this button to do this, press this button to do this.

Help in software environs provides support with respect to using software and in this particular case a means of familiarising students with the 'active' elements of the screens they viewed. The help screen designed provided help with respect to using the software, but it did not help students in terms of clarify concepts, ideas, or beliefs, or in terms of directing them to other related information that may help them understand the science. In hindsight I should have anticipated this as most 'help' buttons on software provide help in terms of using the software. For most educators, help scaffolds understanding of the ideas as well as managing information and learning skills.

The designer in an email communication identified the difficulty in interpreting written specifications and negotiating understanding.

> "Even once the SRS (software requirement specification) was finalised there was some misunderstanding of what was expected." (Designer 1. 19S email)

Written requirements did not result in similar interpretations because words have more than one meaning for those engaged in the design process. Just as the word 'reduction' in everyday language means to get smaller, but in chemistry it means the gain of electrons. In the case of this project, key words meant different things. The transcript on 'help' highlights the importance of the interpretive process. Other words that were interpreted in different ways, include the word constructivist – a key term.

Even though the software requirement specification stated product requirements, interpreting these requirements was achieved with all participants engaged in an interpretive process.

Planning and Designing: The Nature of Interaction

The concept of non-linear access and open pathways was readily interpreted and incorporated. Indeed the opening screen invites users to take ownership of their route through the CDROM.

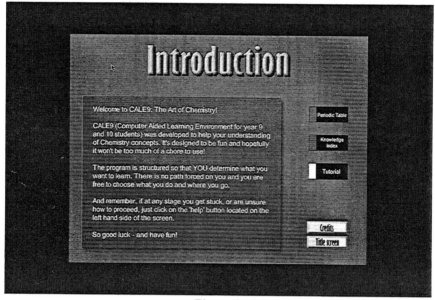

Figure 4

This was further identified by Designer 2 who said:

> "The aim of the CALE (computer assisted learning environment) that we are trying to construct is to assist students to develop their understanding of introductory chemistry concepts. The CALE is to be non-linear and facilitate student-centred exploration of the relevant material ie. the students can examine the material in any order and at their own pace." (2. - email)

This is a common assumption. However, it should be noted, that non-linear software with hyperlinks does not make the software Constructivist, (though it might make it less likely to be seen as Behaviourist). Anyone can still proceed from screen to screen without reflective thought. The role, purpose and nature of interaction within the software were a key discussion point. The designers knew that the development of science concepts required active construction on the part of the learner. The notion of knowledge as a learner's construct is a fundamental aspect of Constructivist learning theory, but it was also a difficult concept for the majority of the designers to interpret. Not surprisingly, a designer said that interpretation of this idea is the client's responsibility:

> "I don't pretend to know how it is children learn. In my role as a software engineer I really consider this the responsibility of the client. I think it is impossible for a software engineer to have a high level of understanding in the subject matter of EVERY project he/she is involved in." (4- email)

The designers knew what was required in terms of scaffolding, but building in appropriate scaffolds was problematic, as was cuing for active engagement on the part of the student. Sharing and interpreting cognitive research findings in the realm of science education so that it results in software reality is challenging. But the designers did note the differences in the nature of interaction possible with standard text resources and the nature of interaction possible with multimedia. For example, Designer 4 said:

> "I would imagine the aim is to provide an experience that a book cannot. Perhaps a computer assisted learning environment may some day replace a human instructor, though I doubt it, but the CALE that WE are endeavouring to create is intended to provide functionality that a book cannot." (4. - email)

But he also recognised that interpreting the wish list requirements of the researcher could be problematic.

> Of course, the possibility that I may misinterpret what the client's views actually are will always exist. But this is a different kettle of fish." (4.- email)

We discussed the construction of a knowledge base, which for me would provide students with support for key ideas. Screen templates were made available for perusal, and it became apparent that the concept of scaffolding conceptual understanding was being interpreted as hands-on interaction for the user. Eventually, after several discussions a notion of active construction became more familiar to the software designers, but even so, to a certain extent active construction manifested itself in the form of 'physical construction' or contrived engagement where users built structures. Constructivist was interpreted as 'construct'. Tasks that enabled students to build 'atoms' were seen as constructivist. This physical construction type interpretation may be due to what is possible with the available technology.

Incorporating minds-on interaction in terms of metacognitive skills and fostering self-questioning was difficult. One designer suggested these concepts were limited by the technology itself. Another constraint in terms of metacognitive skills and self-questioning is the difficulty in interpreting and translating the research findings on cognition into informed response multimedia reality. The designers knew that they were to create a multimedia package that was different to many behaviourist-influenced software and they considered incorporating metacognitive devices such as advance organisers and including frequent decision points while trying not to induce cognitive overload. They considered anchoring concepts by incorporating relevant everyday contexts and they sought to provide help facilities and advice statements. These elements were more complex and not as simple as providing good quality aesthetics, non-linear pathways, quality graphics, open access, and self directed pace.

In designing for navigation ease, we made it relatively easy for students to find responses to questions. They simply went to appropriate screens. For example, if a student is faced with a question pertaining to the atomic number of zinc, the student went to a screen on zinc and read the value. This means that for assessment purposes we need to incorporate questions in the multimedia that do more than access end point information. The nature of the questions and their role in terms of diagnostic or summative assessment should be an important consideration in the development of appropriate multimedia learning environments. Most questions found in software packages involve either a multiple-choice format or a one-word response. The artificial intelligence necessary for interpretation of natural language responses in not widely available. Consequently the role of language, a crucial aspect of constructivist tenets, is not easily accommodated. Most multimedia learning packages serve 'what' type questions, but not 'why' or 'how' type questions. This is one of the fundamental differences between behaviourist and constructivist views of learning.

PLANNING AND DESIGNING: THE ROLE OF SYMBOLS

The designers and I thought that product appearance was important and initially appearance, motivation, non-linear access, and interactiveness were key discussion points between the researcher and designers. The product had multimedia design standards to meet. Therefore font size, style, colour, arrangement of icons, text, and illustrations were important considerations. Even at the conclusion of the project, Designer 3 considered the appearance of the product to be its strength:

> 'The graphics/appearance of the project. Because they are aesthetically pleasing, clear and professional in appearance.' (3. 22S email)

Another aspect in this design phase is the use of appropriate symbols/icons. Science educators influenced by Constructivist views of learning try to provide opportunities for students to accommodate new concepts or modify their existing concepts to match those currently accepted by the scientific community. If we want to influence multimedia theory with constructivist ideology we can either use multimedia as a tool in situated practice (Lave & Wenger, 1991) within a constructivist classroom, or we can incorporate opportunities to facilitate learning. Incorporating a 'facilitator' facet in the software is difficult, as the interactivity will involve use of designer-perceived intuitive icons. Software designers are usually familiar with other multimedia and as a consequence view most icons as intuitive. This is problematic. The excerpts below are taken from a conversation between the designer and I and it illustrates some of the difficulty with respect to perceived clarity of the icons and buttons used in the software.

Verbatim transcript

3:    Disregarding the text below it, what does a pair of binoculars mean to you?
R   I haven't the faintest idea.
2:    Why?
3:    What does this thing that looks like, of course she knows.
R: To you, but it's not to me.
3:    No, it's very intuitive. It looks like a keyboard with an arrow on top.
R: No, I don't know what that means.
3:    And what is this, or that?
R   None of those make sense to me.
3:    Most of these ones are completely understandable.

R: No, no because they come, I'm going to sound really rude, because they come from a programmer's point of view and that is something that you've or they've found common in their context, but it's not common in my context.

3:   Oh no. I just looked at this now and thought what on earth has a pair of binoculars got to do with finding what you are after.

What may often appear obvious to the software engineer is more a consequence of their familiarity with the symbol and its use in other multimedia software rather than an intuitive recognisable representation for a particular action or task. Obviously as icons become standard, their interpretation will become more shared. However at present the development of various icons for the same purpose does not lend itself to ease of interactivity.

DISCUSSION

Most hyperlinked multimedia textbooks (usually CDROMs) are still, in essence, underpinned by behaviourist rather than constructivist views of learning. The behaviourist model sees learning primarily as a process of accumulation, building on what is perceived to be simple and moving to a product which is perceived to be complex. With current multimedia, the notion of non-linear access and, to some degree, autonomy and self-regulation, has been incorporated into software design. But it should be stated that delivering information bytes in a non-linear way does not make multimedia software constructivist. Users, like readers of books, can flick from page to page, that does not make the activity constructivist. Allowing the user access to screens at their own discretion without facilitating active minds-on construction of meaning does not promote metacognition. Metacognitive devices such as advance organisers, concept anchors such as contexts, help buttons, and advice statements, add a form of cognitive overload or could make the system difficult to navigate. In order to use cognitive skills of analysis, synthesis, reconceptualisation, and interpretation, multimedia software must scaffold in order to facilitate minds-on active processing of information. The difficulty at present is that interpreting these scaffolds in terms of multimedia reality is still problematic. Unfortunately this difficulty is compounded by the fact that cognitive research and software designers share nomenclature that has different meanings.

The nature of the influence of educational research on software design is unintentional and in some cases unexpected. To a certain extent, the unexpected influence is due to the fact that conversations have taken place and all feel they have conversed in order to reach a shared and defined goal, only to find they have been talking in parallel contexts. For example, the use of 'help' 'scaffold' or 'constructivist' means different things from different frames of reference. It shouldn't have come as a surprise that educational researcher's notions of active personal construction by the learner were interpreted as hands-on 'construction' by the designers. The learner physically manipulates icons or builds models. This means that minds-on constructivist notions are interpreted as hands-on interactivity.

Particular facets of multimedia have become more prominent in the 1990s and software design has reflected this new potential. These changes in technology are often promoted on the merits of current cognitive psychology, even though many constructivist requirements are difficult to incorporate within existing multimedia. The computer's natural language processing capabilities may limit what a software designer can really do and may often result in users having to provide syntactically accurate responses to any given question. Because the computer cannot interpret partially accurate explanations it produces feedback that is of limited quality to the user. This feedback is a fundamental element of scaffolding. Many constructivist research findings in terms of context, relatedness, and active minds-on engagement in the learning process have yet to be fully interpreted and translated into software design.

The move toward visual operating systems and icon driven menus requires consideration when designing appropriate software for use in school science. When a task is novel, the processes required of that task have not yet been automated, and the user operating the system relies on the clarity of the symbols to help navigate through a programme and make sense of the new ideas.

Not all the symbols are intuitive. Some perceived-to-be-intuitive symbols need clarification. We need to also pay heed to the use of common language that means different things for different agents. We need to find ways of informing multimedia design, at the time of software development, if we really intend to take on board learning theories. Several key advancements and features found in multimedia design draw on contemporary theories of learning, but most of these advancements involve 'hands-on' rather than 'minds-on' elements. Perhaps the technology is still a limiting factor. The challenge for software designers and educational researchers lies in their ability to communicate and discuss issues regarding features of the technology, contemporary views of learning, intended outcomes of the material being developed and the culture in which the material will be used. We need the technology to do more than provide hands-on activity. We need to consider how educational psychology can influence the human computer interface to promote minds on engagement. This will require education researchers and teachers, and software designers to communicate using more explicit dialogue.

REFERENCES

Davidson-Wasser, J & Bresler, L. (1997) Working in the interpretive zone: Conceptualising collaboration in qualitative research teams. *Educational Researcher, 25,* pp5 -15

Dick, W. (1991) An instructional designers view of constructivism. *Educational Technology, 5,* pp41-44

Gagne, R. M. (1970) The conditions of learning. London: Holt Rinehart and Winston.

Hannafin, M.J & Rieber, L. P. (1989) Psychological foundations of instructional design for emerging computer based technologies, *Educational Technology Research and Development, 37,* pp91-101

Heinich, R. (1984) The proper study of instructional technology. *Educational Communication and Technology Journal , 32 ,* pp67-87

Lave, J. & Wenger, E. (1991) *Situated learning: Legitimate peripheral participation.* New York Cambridge University Press.

Lebow, D. (1993) Constructivist values for instructional systems design: Five principles toward a new mindset. *Educational Technology Research and Development , 41,* pp4-16

Liu, M., Jones, C. & Hemstreet, S. (1998) Interactive multimedia design and production processes. *Journal of Research on Computing in Education, 30,* pp254-279

Reigeluth, C. M. (Ed) (1983*) Instructional design theories and models.* Hillsdale, NJ: Lawrence Erlbaum Associates.

Reigeluth, C.M. (1989) Educational technology at the crossroads: New mindsets and new directions. *Educational Technology Research and Development,* 37 (1) pp1042 -1629

Yang, C.S., Moore, D.M., & Burton, J.K. (1995) Managing courseware production: An instructional model with a software engineering approach. *Educational Technology Research and Development, 43,* pp60-70

Vygotsky, L. S. (1962) *Thought and language.* Cambridge, Mass: MIT Press

Vygotsky, L. S. (1978) *Mind in society: The development of higher psychological processes.* Cambridge, Mass: Harvard University Press

THE ZEN OF BEING AN EFFECTIVE MOD

Albert Ip

INTRODUCTION

Breaking away from the "information shoveling" model of online education and training, we need to exploit the communicative power of the Web. Learning need not and should not be a solitary activity. Extending from Jonassen and Reeves' (1996) notion of learning from and learning with the computer, there is a third notion of "learning via" the computer. In this view, computer-mediated communication such as asynchronous conference (AC) has been identified as a teaching space (Hiltz, 1984; Ip, 1989). Researchers (Berge and Collins, 1995; Ip, 1989) identified issues in moderating learning using such systems. In this chapter we explore another strategy, that of online role-play simulations (Linser, 1999; Wills, Ip, and Bunnett, 2000).

A generic classroom provides learning environments for most of the time, however, special purpose learning environments such as science laboratories and dance studios with special designs have a place for special requirements. The online Role-Play Simulation (RPS) described in this chapter is more akin to a specialist environment with embedded pedagogical designs and content supplied by subject matter experts.

The learning occurring within AC is dependent on the skill, effectiveness and dedication of the online moderator. This chapter articulates the underlying pedagogical design for a RPS environment. It also highlights moderation issues for an online role play moderator in capturing and utilising the learning opportunities that occur while maintaining the engaging and fun elements of RPS.

In this chapter, I shall use asynchronous conference, discussion list, and forum loosely as interchangeable terms. Role-play simulation, in this chapter excludes rule-based simulation.   The   person   who   monitors,   supports   and "moderates" with RPS is called the MOD. MOD is used exclusively to refer to the person(s) performing "moderating' activities in an RPS environment. The exact notion of "moderating" in RPS will be explained later in this chapter.

PEDAGOGICAL VIEWPOINTS

This online role play simulation approach promotes "fun" as a key motivator for learning. It focuses on the effective internalisation and transfer of experience created in such a simulated world in order to support future applications of such experiences in real life situations.

Simulations have been used as a tool for teaching in many areas and disciplines. The philosophy underpinning the use of simulations as pedagogical tools relies on an idea that experience is the basis of learning (Ip and Naidu, 2001). If access to such experience in real situations is impossible, expensive or dangerous, an artificial environment may be, if not ideal, at least sufficient to encourage learning. The pedagogy proposed in our RPS design also emphasises the designs that engage and provide fun for learners. RPS have evolved from face to face interaction (such as SimSoc (Gamson, 1966) into using generic email systems such as that reported by Vincent and Shepherd, (1998)) or others using Groupware   products   such   as   Lotus   Notes.   Special   software   supporting specifically designed role-play simulations has also appeared. This chapter is based on Fablusi™, a role-play simulation generator designed by Ip (Ip and Linser, 1999; Ip, Linser, and Naidu, 2001) as a special software environment for web-based online role-play simulations.

In this discussion, there is a constant switch between the "fun" or game aspect of the role-play simulation and the pedagogical aspect in using RPS as a learning environment. A distinction is made between the use of the terms, **goal** and **learning objective** in this chapter. A goal is the "game" objective that the player tries to achieve. The learning objective (sometimes just objective in short) is the objective of pedagogical design - something that the learner may acquire by playing the game or achieving the goal of the game. The terms **role, player** and **learner** are used with care too. A **role** is a persona in the role play simulation and may be played by several participants. The term **player** refers to the participant of the game part. The term **learner** is used to refer to the participant with focus on the pedagogical aspect of the role playing activity.

Linser, Naidu, and Ip, (1999) have listed four essential pedagogical ingredients in using role play in Political Science at an Australian University. The list was based on using RPS as a complimentary strategy to a conventional campus-based course. However the first three of the four points are equally applicable in a totally e-based learning situation. The list is updated here to become the following five ingredients for pure online use of RPS:

- Dynamic goal-based learning;
- Role Play-based learning;
- resources for learning;
- Web-based communication and collaboration, and;
- asynchronicity for reflection and transfer.

Goal-based learning, a form of learning by doing, is a very powerful learning strategy widely acknowledged as a strong motivator for learning. At the core of this strategy is the assumption that knowledge is predicated on the skills by which it is acquired. Thus, the goal for achieving something motivates learning the necessary skills. In other words goals drive the learning process. On the basis of these assumptions, Roger Schank developed what he calls Goal-Based Scenario (GBS) which typically, includes a mission, a cover story, a focus and an operations component (Schank and Cleary, 1995).

For all RPS based on Fablusi™, the pedagogical objectives are not limited to only developing skills, but also to learning about processes, issues, facts and cases. More importantly it is about learning how to analyze these in the context of theories and continuous events. In the study of Law and some other management sciences, knowing and understanding "cases" are an important aspect of the training. Similarly, normative and empirical evaluation of facts and issues, and understanding different approaches, plays a significant part in the pedagogical goals in RPS. These are the 'skills' which some disciplines aim to impart and Fablusi™-based RPS aims to support. Schank and Cleary, (1995) described understanding cases as an 'ambiguous' skill. The RPS design reported in this chapter attempts to achieve the more 'ambiguous' goals from which Shank shies away.

RPS specifically integrates GBS into a more flexible delivery mechanism with moderator intervention capability. Therefore what Schank calls 'missions' and 'cover story' (initial and context scenario) need not remain given or fixed. Rather, given the role interactive capacity of the simulation, the 'cover story' can be responsive to the actions taken by the roles. Role interaction produces effects which feedback into the 'cover story' and thus demand attention from the players to respond. In effect, there is a continuously fluctuating and changing scenario context - a 'dynamic scenario'. GBS has only one mission because typically, a GBS has only one playable role. In RPS, each role may have a different mission or role agenda.

The effect on the learning process (by this transformation of static scenario context into a dynamic scenario) are that

1. the activities of the student rather than the teacher drive the learning;
2. there is a constant demand on the player to evaluate the new situation and this provides ample learning opportunities for
   - acquiring the knowledge as represented by the game context (e.g. historical facts and issues as in role play of the first fleet: historically significant events and the issues faced by the first group of western settlers in Australia)
   - trying out and pragmatic executing of strategy (e.g. in political science simulation where learners playing political leaders trying to drive the agenda of that persona)
   - evaluating theories
3. it demonstrates that the importance of knowing cases, events and facts, is determined by how they are generated and used.

The second critical ingredient of this simulation design is play - in the sense of playing a role, playing with possibilities and alternative worlds, and playing for fun. The strategy of learning through playing is significant, not least because 'having fun' in the process of learning is an extremely powerful motivator. More importantly, it gives students a personal stake in the proceedings and hence potentially a reflexive learning process is initiated by these proceedings. The ownership of a role by the player is an important aspect of this design which an MOD must understand.

The third critical ingredient is the "traditional" teaching function of RPS. One of the key differences between our RPS as a learning environment and role playing as a game is the different emphasis in learning and entertainment between these uses. When role-play is used as a game, the emphasis is on its engaging ability and entertainment value. Any move by the player is not to be analysed later in any debrief. Any learning, for example a consequence of research done by game players and later transferred into skills and knowledge a game player may apply in a real life situation, is circumstantial and a by-product. However, as a learning environment, this type of agenda is a focus of the design. As a learner faces challenges within the RPS environment, it is important to provide resources, case studies, theories and/or alternatives to support the learning aspects of the design. These provisions are intended to encourage learning.

The World Wide Web provides a virtual space for communication, information and collaboration among learners, and between the learners/players and MOD in synchronous and asynchronous modes. The Web also enables access to resources, such as current news from electronic newspapers and web-sites from all over the world as well as access to moderators (facilitators, mentors or control as called by different authors) as and when they need them.

The asynchronous nature of RPS provides time for players to consider alternatives, and research or use "out-of-simulation" discussions before making a "move". However, it could also be argued that "the ability to rapidly respond to situation" may be a valid learning objective for many situations. As a learning environment, RPS is a good environment to explore possibilities, establish strategies, promote confidences and evaluate consequences for any response and to anticipate making rapid responses in real life situations. In other words, RPS provides the practice necessary to make rational and considered responses for future need of rapid response. This "just-in-case" training is an important part of emergency and crisis preparedness and has been overlooked in the recent emphasis on the economic rationalistic "just-in-time" training philosophy promoted by some online training vendors.

Many experienced on-line educators (Brown, 1998; Durham, 1998; Hedberg and Harper, 1998; Price, 1998) have emphasized the importance of including face to face interaction in teaching with the aid of Computer Mediated Communication and online teaching. The importance of incorporating these techniques into the face to face interaction with asynchronous conference is not simply for their utility in the presentation of facts, cases and theories, they also provide communicative events that stimulate reflection about actions undertaken and strategies pursuit, by comparing real world events with the simulated ones. The use of face to face opportunities in a course incorporating RPS may be mainly for debriefing because online role play simulation, when designed correctly, can provide resources in a more timely manner (on demand) and the rich communication structure and the asynchronicity would have provided ample opportunities for reflection and evaluation of actions taken.

The online mode, with the ability to provide anonymity, has an added value for adult learners who may find it difficult to role play in a face to face situation. The lack of richness in online communication can be leveraged to encourage ownership of roles and imagination of players, enhancing the entertainment value of RPS.

ONLINE ROLE PLAY SIMULATION

Figure 1 shows the structure of RPS. Central to RPS are the roles. The RPS creator would have already

- consolidated the stakeholders viewpoints into a set of roles,
- create the scenario by using different types of information for the roles,
- set up the social structure among the roles based on the information differences, availability of sim-conference and the rights of those available conference

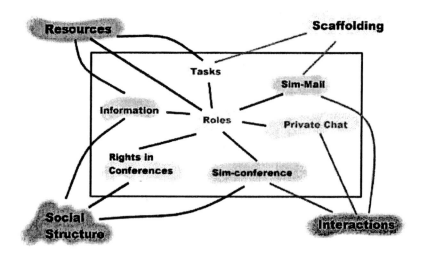

Figure 1 Role-Play Simulation Features

The RPS creator may also have provided an RPS manual to the MOD including the learning objectives embedded by the design, the kick-up episode and other relevant background resources, case studies and/or examples to support learning. The focus of the MOD is to ensure the smooth running and the effectiveness of the learning environment during RPS.

INTERACTIONS

The roles engage and pursue their agenda (goals) via three forms of communication. These are:

- a sim-mail subsystem for any role to send messages to any other *role* (similar to email), and/or
- sim-conferences, and
- real time chat rooms.

The sim-mail is very similar to email. However, since it is not a "real" email system, *roles* can only communicate with other *roles* by selecting role names in the recipient list. The real name of the player is not recognized by the system. The MOD should monitor all messages passing through the sim-mail subsystem.

The sim-conference reflects the various kinds of forums found in politics, commercial and other environments. Messages in sim-conferences do not address a particular role, however the sender of the message may be identified automatically. Fablusi™ Sim-conference is implemented differently from most other asynchronous conferences in that it supports various "document types" which provides some social structure. The MOD can read, create and edit any message of any document type within all sim-conferences.

Instead of running chat rooms continuously, the Fablusi™ implementation only provides private chat rooms for roles to book and use. The booking creates private chat room only for those roles who have the key to enter. The key is distributed by the sim-mail subsystem. At the time booked, roles with the key can enter the chat room by clicking on the key. While the MOD will also receive the "invitation to chat", the MOD is not expected to monitor all private chat rooms.

Task

Fablusi™ RPS is driven by "tasks". Both simulation creator and the MOD can set "tasks" for specific *roles*. These tasks can have time limits. When a role completes a task, the result of the task may become available to other *roles*. For example, a task may be the writing of a *role profile*. As the role submits the profile, it will be available to all other roles to read automatically.

The MOD can use tasks as scaffolding devices guiding *roles* progressively towards the final overall goal of the game and create the necessary learning experience. When necessary, tasks can also be used for assessment purposes.

Player Tool: NotePad

Players have access to notepads which enable shared roles. Because both the sim-mail and sim-conference are inter-role communication mechanisms, when a role is played by more than one learner, it becomes necessary to enable a common area where a team (playing the same *role*) may share some private information (e.g. strategies for playing the game). The notepad is private to the *role*, MOD cannot read the information on the notepad.

DIFFERENCES IN MODERATING ASYNCHRONOUS CONFERENCES AND ONLINE ROLE PLAY SIMULATIONS

What happens in a classroom depends to a certain extent on the pedagogical inclination of the teacher. These inclinations are based on teachers' philosophical orientations and theories regarding education. In general, effective teaching through AC relies on a learner-centered approach, it rests on principles of collaborative learning and egalitarian relationships (Eastmond, 1992; Florini, 1989; Harasim, 1989; Kaye, 1989). Effective discussion requires that everyone involved, instructor and students alike, share in both the teaching and the learning. All participants assume responsibility for furthering discussion, although students may require special preparation and clear guidelines to participate effectively (Rohfeld and Hiemstra, 1995). Face-to-face classroom discussion groups and public electronic discussion groups have similarities. They all are social activities and involve discussion. They are cooperative endeavors, usually rational and purposeful, sometimes systematic and often creative. They require participation, involve formal/informal leadership or moderation (Hyman, 1980, pp. 13-17) and are used by their participants as venues for formal and informal learning (Collins and Berge, 1996).

The Fablusi™ platform provides a learning environment with embedded pedagogical underpinnings. RPS on Fablusi™ platform is a role-play simulation with embedded content created by subject matter experts. Hence it is believed that the pedagogical inclination of the MOD in RPS has less influence on learning when compared to the influence of the moderator in AC. In general, effective learning in RPS also relies on a learner-centered approach resting on principles of collaborative and co-operative learning and structured relationships. Effective game progression requires that every role meet the "participation obligation" of role-playing. If a role with a critical stakeholder viewpoint does not participate effectively, it is difficult for the whole RPS to explore issues related to that particular viewpoint. *Participation obligation* is a term used to describe the requirement of players to participate with regular frequency and involvement. This is usually set as a "hurdle" requirement and must be communicated to players before they are assigned a role in the RPS. Once drawn into the 'game play', players usually need no further inducement to enforce "participation obligation". The MOD may have to monitor whether a role spends too much time in just one RPS and upsets the balance of a real life situation.

ENVIRONMENT FACTORS

In an online asynchronous conference, sarcasm and wit takes on new meaning and has the potential to be misunderstood (Loughlin, 1993). Without members of a group having prior knowledge of each other, the status brought by an imposing physical appearance, a loud tone of voice, or a title, doesn't translate on-line, removing the normal structure of face to face communication and making communication different and sometimes difficult. Miscommunication, loss of status, inhibition, and not seeing others as full and real people can lead to the following problems in an educationally oriented AC.

- Lack of participation
- Lack of focus
- Monopolization of a topic
- Lack of anything greater than surface discourse
- Deferring to previous authors by adding nothing more than 'I agree'
- Personal verbal attacks directed at individual group members
- Use of inappropriate language and online behavior
- Instigation of arguments between participants
- Early dry-out of discussion ideas

By contrast, the learners, taking on a persona in the role play simulation, would be interacting in character. There is an implied social structure in the RPS as designed by the subject matter expert. After the initial period of familarisation of the role, the many issues faced by AC generally disappear. As different roles are representing different stakeholders and are in active pursuit of that stakeholder's interest, it is unlikely that a single player will dominate communication. The use of response such as 'I agree' usually does not help much in advancing the cause of the role in RPS and hence has rarely appeared in the numerous simulation logs in our projects. Use of language is also dictated by the role status. It is interesting to note the change and different use of language by players in the RPS. Most players will use a language appropriate to the role within the RPS game environment and a different language in the out-of-simulation communication with his/her partner as evident in the role notepad. As the role play progresses, the dynamic nature of the scenario manifests naturally, and provides new or adjusted agendas for the roles to pursue. Early dry-out of discussion ideas leading to limited communication never occurred in any of the RPS projects we have run. However, the change of perceived sarcasm and wit must be acknowledged as players are still working in an online environment and suffer the same limited "band width" issue.

ROLE OF MODERATOR/MOD

Mason (1991) identifies three role functions that AC moderators must provide. These role functions are:

- **Organizational role**: set the agenda and objectives of the discussion, the timetable, procedural rules and decision-making norms.
- **Social role:** create a friendly, social environment for learning, especially encourage participation using a friendly, personal tone
- **Teaching role:** facilitate learning by focussing discussions on crucial points, asking questions and probing responses to encourage students to expand and build on comments. (Mason, 1991)

In a RPS, the player determines the agenda for each role. MOD needs to ensure that the public and private agenda put forward by the role are consistent with the role specific information provided to the role by the subject matter expert who designed the RPS. The progression of the game of RPS depends on the participation obligation agreed by the players before the start of RPS. The decision-making rules are again determined by the rules set by the simulation author in various sim-conferences as role rights.

While MOD may send an initial message to the players welcoming them to play RPS, normally, there will be little need to continue to function in a social role as identified by Mason. The use of friendly and personal tones in the welcome message is instrumental in promoting active engagement.

A MOD operation in RPS requires the following facets:

- **Guardian angel:** MOD can read most communications between roles in the RPS. With this ability, MOD watches players' moves and must maintain an overview of the general direction of the game progression. MOD needs to Help when something goes wrong, or a role is not advancing satisfactorily and though they must respond to help requests from the player they must judge and provide or decline requests based on the learning objectives set in the RPS. While the MOD should communicate a sense of support to the roles, it is important that roles do not become over dependent on the MOD to advance the game progression.

  "Duty of care" is a notion commonly mentioned and practiced by teachers of younger children. Some role play simulations are psychologically intense and it is important that the MOD understands the risk and likelihood of mixing the virtual world with real world. While we like to see transfer of experience from the simulated world into real world, it is critically important that players do not confuse actions in the simulated world (especially violent actions) with available actions in a real world. In the simulated world, some actions are allowed as a means to study and evaluate the consequence of such action. Some of these actions may be morally unacceptable or illegal in the real world. The MOD must ensure that players understand the purpose in allowing these actions to happen in the simulated world.

- **Manipulative devil:** One tactic to create learning is to set up problems for roles to solve. These problems can be inserted into RPS by "setting up" the player as in leaking critical game information to the role's opponent or creating difficult situations when things are going smoothly. RPS based on Fablusi™ does not have any random elements. If there is a natural disaster occurring in a game, it is NOT a random act. It is either set up by the simulation creator or inserted into the game play by the MOD. As such, the MOD is a manipulative devil.

- **Resident educator/learner:** To ensure role playing is a learning activity instead of just a game or entertainment, the MOD needs to recognise learning opportunities. The MOD promotes learning opportunities into potential learning by providing suggestions (more than one) or highlighting relevant theory and resources to the roles. Just in time resources or hints are good strategies too. The MOD should promote reflection and consideration of alternatives. When suggesting alternatives it is important to ensure that the player takes responsibility for his/her own action. Since RPS fits well with domains where there are no black and white answers, the MOD should keep an open mind. Even actions which seem unlikely to occur should be allowed either for the sake of "what-if" testing or for the sake of creating counter examples which are useful when debriefing.

- **Improvising story teller:** Sometimes unforeseen game situations will require additional scenario modification or extensions. The MOD becomes a story teller and creates extensions to the original design to cater for the situation.

- **An administrator:** MOD provides guidance and solves technical issues, sets up tasks for roles and *reverses tasks* if players have wrongly committed to the tasks. The MOD also needs to delete wrong or duplicated messages in sim-conferences Enforcing "participation obligation" may also be classified as an administrator's task.

LIFE CYCLE OF ROLE PLAYING

Like any work group, learners in RPS need to rapidly establish a work pattern to engage with the game and the experience building exercise. Understanding the life cycle of RPS helps the MOD to operate more effectively.

Pre-play

As the name suggests, this is a stage before RPS actually begins. The length of this stage will depend on participants' familiarity with RPS. The MOD must build trust relationship with the players, remove technical anxieties, identify role selection and explain game rules.

- **Trust relationship:** Since role playing is a dramatically and emotionally charged environment, it is important for players to trust the MOD in order to participate effectively in the role play. The MOD should, at this stage, explain to the players that the MOD will be acting like a guardian angel and would provide help whenever necessary. However, the MOD must stress that the player must be responsible for the action of the role and since it is a simulation, such actions can be taken in the view of generating experience for learning purposes.

- **Technical anxieties:** Potential players need to overcome technical anxieties such as establishing internet connectivity, accessing the web site and understanding the available features. Demonstration of a small RPS usually overcomes these technical anxieties quickly. Another requirement which should be communicated clearly to potential players is the requirement of "participation obligation". This seeks the players' commitment to this obligation throughout the intended period when RPS will be running (including the debriefing stage). It is better to have frequent short connections than long but infrequent connections. RPS is 'quasi-asynchronous". Players can participate at any time of the day (asynchronous). In order to maintain the richness of the experience, all stakeholders' views should be explored. This requires the game to advance in steps with full participation of all roles. If one role fails to participate, other roles may be affected and hence the need for "participation obligation".

- **Role selection:** Potential players, after agreeing to the participation obligation, need to submit preferred roles based on minimum role information. Typically, the role information will only include role names and possibly a job title. At this stage, it is important that the private agenda given to the role be kept secret so that meaningful communication and interaction among roles can occur during the development stage.

- **Game rules:** While technically Fablusi™ will support sim-mail with an unlimited number of recipients, it would be a good idea to establish a maximum number of recipients in each sim-mail. In the real world, a role cannot broadcast to the whole world. When a role would like to take a "violent" action which may limit the ability of other roles to participate, the permission of the MOD is required. Game rules like these are NOT enforced by the underlying software and depend on the MOD to make them clear to the roles. These game rules must be explained to players at this stage.

Early Stage

Time spent in this stage can be very rewarding later. This stage requires a fair amount of research and writing for the learners.

- **Understand role:** Simulation designers (subject matter experts) deliberately create only sketchy descriptions of the roles. This is to promote the ownership of the role by allowing learners/players to embellish the character, research the stakeholder viewpoints and establish operational public and private agenda. At this stage, learners should be told their assigned roles and begin to research and write up a *role profile* for other roles to read. A fixed date for posting the role profile will establish the quasi-asynchronous nature. This date may match the date when the MOD releases the initial kick-start episode of the scenario. The public agenda of the role can be published as part of the role profile, however, the MOD may request the players to send the private agenda as sim-mail to the MOD. There is a significant learning opportunity at this stage and the MOD may choose to make the write up of the role profile part of the assessment.
- **Understand scenario and engage:** In the second part of this stage, roles need to have a compelling reason to act. The MOD releases the kick-start episode of the scenario. One design objective of the kick-start episode is to create compelling reasons for sufficient number of roles to act immediately. As roles are engaged, the MOD needs to start monitoring the sim-mail and sim-conference regular and exercise the various MOD duties.

Development:

This is the key stage of the experience building process. For a RPS lasting for 4 weeks, this stage may start at the beginning of the second week and will last for about 2 weeks. The duration should depend on the complexity of the issue and the frequency of connection in the agreed participation obligation.

- **Understand issues:** During the early part of this stage, roles need to understand the issues and formulate a strategy to achieve and advance the roles' public and private agenda. Understanding issues may include researching, reading cases, sharing experiences both within and outside the simulation. A lot of the "traditional" learning functions occur at this stage. However the strength of RPS as a learning environment is the ability for the roles to execute (practice) the strategy and try to advance the roles' agenda in a safe environment in the later part of this stage.
- **Pursuit agenda:** Roles interact in order to pursue their public and private agenda using the various communication channels available in RPS. They

will be using tactics such as forming alliances, explaining positions, threats or exercising legal rights. MOD is now the guardian angel, the manipulative devil, the resident learner/educator, improvising story teller and the administrator. The focus is to allow roles to experience and have time to consider every move.

These are some of the most powerful features of RPS as a learning environment: building experience while having time to reflect on each move. Case-based learning provides ample opportunities to understand issues, and discuss and debate possible strategies. RPS integrates the unique opportunity for roles to execute the strategy and advance the roles' agenda. Learners are motivated to study various cases and use them as guides or examples (or counter examples). They also have ample time to research best approaches to tackle the issues or advance the roles' agenda.

Debriefing, Assessment and Evaluation

This final stage is an important stage of the whole RPS experience.

Disengage: After playing a character for two weeks or more, the player will be thinking and acting as a role within the RPS. One of the key objectives of this stage is to disengage and help the players re-engage in the real world. We cannot stress the importance of disengagement. It is very important that a player realises the difference between the simulated world and the real world and applies rational control over the experience in order to learn.

Reflect and learn: RPS is a virtual environment designed to create experience and learning opportunities. However, it is important to help transfer this experience so that it can be used to influence decision making, alter behaviour and change attitudes.

To help achieve these points, the MOD can suggest that players reflect

- from the 'roles' point of view on how the role has performed in the simulation
- from the players' own point of view how the player has made the role lively, effective and faithful to the stakeholder viewpoint, and
- from an observers point of view.

The learner should try to step back and take an objective view, trying to compare any theory with the activities within the role play. It is important that such reflection is encouraged and that it is done without bias or defense as a persona in the role play nor as the player.

CONCLUSION

For the most part, universities and schools continue to pursue teaching with little awareness of pedagogy. We continue to teach the way we were taught, after all we have been successful, so the system must work! Our didactic practices continue to reinforce students' views of learning in which students are passive recipients of teacher delivered factual information. However, with the widespread incorporation of technology in learning environments, the "old" approaches will not promote the skills, literacies and competence now required by our changing world. We should not shy away from experimenting with new ways of engaging our learners, or promoting new skills, and we should be proud to shift away from the "information shoveling" model of online education and training.

The last couple of decades have seen revolutionary changes in the way we access and manage information. There has been an explosive increase in our ability to communicate and there is a pervasive use of technology in all walks of life. Since the early days of the PLATO experiment, computing technology has been promising revolutionary change within education. We are yet to witness such revolutionary change. However, the integration of communication with computation opens up new potential and opportunity. We need to question the wisdom of an online training/learning model in which learners work alone in front of the computer, albeit just-in-time and, anytime, anywhere.

Faced with such opportunities from the technology revolution, we need to refresh our pedagogical beliefs to capture these opportunities. Millions of people are engaged in role playing as a way of entertainment. We engaged in role play when we were young, pretending to be fathers, mothers, cooks and other imaginative roles and we learnt a lot from this early role play. John Dewey's observation, that "true learning is based on discovery guided by mentoring rather than the transmission of knowledge" (cited in Boyer 1998, p.15) is supported by Ip's work on the development of on-line role play simulations. This work is also inline with current pedagogical beliefs such as problem-based and learner-centered constructivist views of learning. In a way, online role play simulation is online problem based learning where participants adopt 'roles' and engage in a 'simulation'. The separation of role play as a game and role play as a learning environment depends to a large extent on the MOD. The MOD, in a way, is Dewey's "mentor".

Role play does not necessarily focus on the final solution to the problem, rather, it should be seen as the process of understanding the issues, developing strategy to handle the problem and accepting alternate views forwarded by other stakeholders while advancing the agenda of the role.

As in the real world, the problems and situations evolve. The role play simulation acknowledges the fact that the nature of the problem can change as the 'roles' delineate aspects they understand and don't understand and the MOD galvanises, when needed, direction and new action. The very presence of the 'roles' changes the nature of the simulation as each role brings to the simulation individuality and viewpoints backed by appropriate research.

REFERENCE

Berge, Z. L., and Collins, M. P. (Eds.) (1995) *Computer-mediated communication and the on-line classroom in Distance Education.* Cresskill, NJ: Hampton Press.

Brown, M. (1998, 27-30 September,) *Teacher for a New Age: The Myths and realities of the Global Classroom.* Paper presented at the *Apple University Consortium Conference.* University of Melbourne.

Boyer (1998). Educating Undergraduates Reinventing Undergraduate Education: A Blueprint for America's Research Universities. (HREF http://notes.cc.sunysb.edu/Pres/boyer.nsf/webform/images/$File/boyer.txt) checked16th February, 2002.

Collins, M. P., and Berge, Z. L. (1996, October 24-26, 1996.) *Mailing lists as a venue for adult learning.* Paper presented at the Eastern Adult, Continuing and Distance Education Research Conference. Pennsylvania State University.

Durham, M. (1998, 27-30 September,) *Working at Virtual Records - a simulated workplace.* Paper presented at the *Apple University Consortium Conference.* University of Melbourne.

Eastmond, D. V. (1992) Effective facilitation of computer conferencing. *Continuing Higher Education Review, 56,* pp155-167.

Florini, B. (1989) Teaching styles and technology. In E. R. Hayes (Ed.), *Effective teaching styles (New Directions for Adult and Continuing Education* (Vol. 43, pp. 41-53). San Francisco: Jossey-Bass.

Gamson, W. (1966) *SimSoc: Participant's Manual with Selected Readings.* New York: The Free Press.

Harasim, L. (1989) Online education: A new domain. In R. Mason and A. Kaye (Eds.), *Mindweave: Communication, computers, and distance education* (pp. 5-62). Oxford, UK: Pergamon Press.

Hedberg, J., and Harper, B. (1998, 27-30 September,) *Supporting flexible thinking with interactive multimedia.* Paper presented at the *Apple University Consortium Conference.* University of Melbourne.

Hiltz, S. R. (1984) *Online Community.* New Jersey: Ablex Publishing Corporation.

Hyman, R. T. (1980) *Improving Discussion Leadership.* New York: Teachers College Press.

Ip, A. (1989) *A Study of the Potential of Electronic Bulletin Boards as Perceived by Teachers.* Unpublished M.Ed, The University of Hong Kong, Hong Kong.

Ip, A., and Linser, R. (1999) Web-based Simulation Generator: Empowering Teaching and Learning Media in Political Science. http://www.roleplaysim. org/papers/rpsg.htm.

Ip, A., Linser, R., and Naidu, S. (2001, 22nd - 25th April 2001) *Simulated Worlds: Rapid Generation of Web-Based Role-Play.* Paper presented at the AusWeb01, Novotel Opal Cove Resort, Coffs Harbour.

Ip, A., and Naidu, S. (2001) Experienced-Based Pedagogical Designs for eLearning. *Education Technology, XLI(5),* pp53-58.

Jonassen, D. H., and Reeves, T. C. (1996) Learning with technology: Using computers as cognitive tools. In D. H. Jonassen (Ed.), *Handbook of research for educational communications and technology* pp693-719. New York: Macmillan.

Kaye, A. (1989) Computer-mediated communication and distance education. In R. Mason and A. Kaye (Eds.), *Mindweave: Communication, computers, and distance education* pp. 3-21. Oxford, UK: Pergamon Press.

Linser, R., Naidu, S., and Ip, A. (1999) *Pedagogical Foundations of Web-based Simulations in Political Science.* Paper presented at the ASCILITE, University of Wollongong, Wollongong, NSW, Australia.

Linser, R. N., S. (1999) *Web-based Simulations As Teaching And Learning Media In Political Science.* Paper presented at the AusWeb99.

Loughlin, T. W. (1993) VIRTUAL RELATIONSHIPS: THE SOLITARY WORLD OF CMC. *Interpersonal Computing and Technology: An Electronic Journal for the 21st Century, 1*(1).

Mason, R. (1991). "Moderating Educational Computer Conferencing." DEOSNEWS 1 (19).

Price, B. A. (1998, 27-30 September) *From global scalable distance teaching to high Bandwidth classroom resources in local schools.* Paper presented at the *Apple University Consortium Conferenc*e. University of Melbourne.

Rohfeld, R. W., and Hiemstra, R. (1995) Moderating Discussions in the Electronic Classroom. In Z. L. Berge and M. P. Collins (Eds.), *Computer-mediated communication and the on-line classroom in Distance Education.* Cresskill, NJ: Hampton Press.

Schank, R. C., and Cleary, C. (1995) *Engines for Education.* Hillsdale, NJ: Lawrence Erlbaum Associates Publishers.

Vincent, A., and Shepherd, J. (1998) Experiences in Teaching Middle East Politics via Internet-based Role-Play Simulations. *Journal of Interactive Media in Education,*(11).

Wills, S., Ip, A., and Bunnett, A. (2000) *Complementary Pedagogical Strategies for Online Design.* Paper presented at the 17th Annual Conference of the Australasian Society for Computers in Learning in Tertiary Education, Coffs Harbour NSW Australia.

MINDFULNESS AND MINDLESSNESS WHEN USING VIDEO-ANALYSIS AND DATA LOGGERS IN TERTIARY PHYSICS PRACTICAL WORK

Susan Rodrigues

INTRODUCTION

In recent years, two of the most commonly found technologies in science learning environments are data loggers and CDROMS. These technologies seem to have found a niche within these environments because they are perceived to add another dimension to the learning experience or enhance the existing experience. But to what extent and how these technologies influence understanding has still to be fully explained.

If we accept that understanding is more than the sum knowledge one has about something (White, 1992) and that it includes the mental process in which relationships are inferred from and between information, then understanding involves the creation and storage of schema. A schema as Fiske and Taylor (1984) suggest, is "a cognitive structure that represents organised knowledge about a given concern or type of stimulus". These schema are stored data, labelled with emotion, attitudes, beliefs and 'knowing' and they are constantly being built in order to guide each individual's actions. The construction of schema is cued by external contexts in which the original data/information is experienced. The reconstruction of new cognitive schema will depend upon how intelligible and fruitful relationships and elements from the old schema are, in terms of assimilating or integrating new information. Therefore, new concrete experiences could through reflection result in new schema formation (Korthagen and Lagerwerf 1995) or new concrete experiences could result in old schema being reinforced. This chapter provides snapshots of some students' approaches to internalising concrete experiences when using dataloggers or video analysis when undertaking tertiary physics practical work.

In the teaching and learning of physics, we promote the use of practical work in order to provide concrete experiences that can be explored, investigated, challenged and supported, with a view to encouraging learning of accepted science concepts, skills and processes. Even though Hodson (1992, 1996, 1998) indicated that practical work in school science has several objectives: to keep students busy; to keep students interested, and to teach them science concepts or skills, he has also shown that practical work is problematic. Yet we continue to promote practical work, and the majority of physics students engage in practical work which involves making some observations and drawing directed inferences from their observations. However, Kirschner and Huisman (1998) suggest that viewing undergraduate laboratory work as an opportunity to help illustrate theory, provide meaningful learning, and provide an insight into phenomena, is flawed. They suggest that laboratory work provides poor 'return of knowledge' for the time used and they suggest that non-trivial experiments may overwhelm students. In recent times the use of certain information communication technology (ICT) has been promoted in terms of being able to simplify the complexity and routine of science (see for example, Rogers 1990; Scaife 1993).

Not surprisingly, several of the concrete experiences commonly encountered in practical work in school and higher education have come to involve the use of ICT. In this chapter I illustrate how concrete experiences involving the use of ICT enable tertiary students to develop and support their understanding of physics concepts encountered in practical work. I illustrate how the use of ICT in practical work could resolve some of the problems identified by Hodson (1992, 1996) and create other problems. In particular I focus on what Langer (1993) terms mindlessness and mindfulness. Mindlessness is when the learner fails to take into account versions of information that might be more fruitful in the future. Mindfulness takes into account distinctions and considers information from different perspectives (Langer, 1993). To what extent does the students' use of ICT determine their mindfulness and mindlessness and hence the adequacy of their existing science understandings?

For Mingers (1995), the object of our knowledge does not exist except as the observer distinguishes it. In this way mindfulness and mindlessness when it comes to examining information from new perspectives is crucial in the development of schema. The push to use ICT will have to take into account the learning environment, the learner's goal, and the situation in which they find themselves and their determination of the adequacy of their existing understandings. These are all critical factors in determining mindfulness and mindlessness.

Students' dispositions and consequently their mindfulness and mindlessness, are thought to have significant impact on their learning, or learning capacity. As Bourdieu (1992; 16) said '...the active presence of past experiences, which, deposited in each organism in the form of schemes of perception, thought and action, tend to guarantee the 'correctness' of practices and their constancy over time, more reliably than all formal rules and explicit norms' . This view is further endorsed by Langer (1993) who suggests that learners do not reconsider what they mindlessly accept as true.

The investigation reported in this chapter focused on learning strategies used by tertiary students working on a first-year physics laboratory exercise involving the analysis of real-life motion activities using either a data logger or video analysis of a simulation. In this chapter I describe some of the findings, and focus specifically on how the student's goals, the situations in which they find themselves and their determination of the adequacy of their existing understandings help them make sense of the science they encounter.

Given that this project hinges on the use of specific ICT in practical work, I begin by reviewing the argument and rationale for using dataloggers and simulations in science in practical work in science and then follow this with a description of the project. I conclude with an exploration and discussion of the findings.

WHY USE DATALOGGERS IN LABORATORY WORK?

Data loggers link a computer to sensors or probes in order to measure, present and analyse data. They are being marketed widely for use in science classrooms. Argument to use data loggers include a perception that they would: reduce the monotony of repetitive experiments (see Rodrigues 1997); enhance learning of intended concepts because they limit distracters; avoid measurement activities that warrant complex calculations; allow for experiments with 'too fast or too slow' measurements; have credibility because it is high tech (Rogers 1990; Scaife 1993). Another advantage is the fact that data loggers provide instant presentations of the collected data.

In science practical work, experiments on the topic of Motion can be designed to involve dataloggers. Students would not have to cut and paste strands of paper with a given number of dots in order to establish velocity graphs, as dataloggers could replace ticker tape. Data-loggers in motion experiments could shift student focus from the manipulation of strips of paper, usually found in tickertape experiments, to the analysis of the patterns observed in the graphed data. Many teachers are accustomed to students experiencing difficulty in understanding ticker tape data, because the exercise for some students becomes one of deciphering code rather than a study of motion (Scaife, 1993).

The belief that datalogging experiments enhance students' understanding of science concepts while addressing issues of repetition in graph drawing (Linn and Songer, 1991) and promotes knowledge of science concepts and processes (Summers, Solomon, Bevan, Frost, Reynolds, and Zimmerman, 1991) has probably increased the use of dataloggers in science classrooms. There is some debate about de-skilling students as a consequence of not requiring them to plot graphs, but as Coleman (1996) suggests, recognising relationships and developing understanding is a fundamental aspect in learning science, and plotting graphs may be limiting the development of student potential. Newton (1997) documented how a group of students engaged in real time data collection and graphing were able to develop skills that enabled them to identify trends and patterns. The students also used vocabulary that gave the data some dynamicism. Not surprisingly, given these views, data loggers are being promoted for use in teaching and learning science.

WHY USE SIMULATIONS IN LABORATORY WORK?

The use of ICT in science lessons has also been argued on the grounds of safety and cost and as a consequence simulations have rapidly gained prominence in practical work. Simulations can be used for hypothetical experiments; those normally impractical due to cost, safety, access, magnitude or time constraints (Steed 1992) or because they break the laws of nature (Scanlon, O'Shea, Smith, Taylor and O'Malley 1993). Simulations could also be used for tidy experiments or for instrumental data capture (Scanlon, et al 1993), when simulations work with sensors to provide the real time data which can then be plotted and explored. In addition, simulations could be used for mathematical modelling, where the students alter laws or provide the data, (Scanlon, et al 1993). There is also ample research documenting student use of dissection simulations. For example, it has been reported that students using a simulation dissection programme to prepare for dissection were more competent in dissection experiments than their counterparts who had received no prior help or had viewed a video which showed dissection preparation (Kinzie et al,1993).

The effectiveness of video in what and how science is learned in contrast to real, hands-on laboratory experiences is continually debated. To some extent the debate has only recently been extended to determining the effectiveness of ICT in learning. A discussion of the debate on using microcomputer-based and video-based resources can be found in Beichner (1990), Escalada & Zollman (1996), Redish, Saul & Steinberg (1997).

WHY INVESTIGATE DATALOGGERS AND SIMULATIONS IN TERTIARY LABORATORY WORK?

I became aware of work conducted by Jon Pearce and Michelle Livett in the late 1990s and knew that they had already undertaken a project aimed at developing an on-line resource for teaching physics to first year undergraduate students. Jon's Real World Physic project allowed students to record position data frame-by-frame from a video-clip and then explore this through an on-line spreadsheet and graphical representation. The data could be viewed on-screen as video, spreadsheets or graphical data and it was linked in such as way as to enable changes in one representation to automatically update changes in other presentation modes. More information regarding Jon's projects and the use of data loggers in motion experiments can be found in Pearce (1993).

Jon and Michelle's project resources enabled me to pursue my agenda and gain a better understanding of the way undergraduate students used ICT to help them make sense of concepts of motion when they complete a laboratory activity using either video analysis or data loggers. In this chapter I focus on how some undergraduate students' interact with computer-based video-analysis tools and dataloggers. I consider their mindfulness and mindlessness when working with dataloggers where software displays graphs of position, velocity and acceleration in real time or when working with computer-based video-analysis tools that allow frame-by-frame basis analysis. I worked with Jon and Michelle on this project and we have reported on some of the findings previously (for further details see Rodrigues, Pearce and Livett, 2000). Jon and Michelle were involved in teaching undergraduate physics and the use of data loggers was normal practice in their subject.

Students used data loggers to record graphs of the motion of objects. The students could move the object near an ultrasonic data logger interfaced to a computer which would display graphs in real time as position, speed or acceleration versus time graphs. In Jon and Michelle's lab, students were randomly assigned to two motion laboratory exercises. They could use the ultrasonic datalogger to collect data in real time while pushing carts, or manually conducting the experiment. Alternatively, students could use the video analysis tool that had objects on screen. The students would manipulate the video representations on screen.

The main concepts promoted in the data logging and video analysis laboratory activities were:

- relationships between velocity and acceleration graphs,
- the effects of a constant external force acting on an object,
- the motion of an object projected vertically into the air.

Some of the Project Details

The students involved in the project were first year undergraduate students. The video analysis method was not a usual part of laboratory activity, but the use of dataloggers had already been incorporated into laboratory work at first year undergraduate level. However, it should be noted that at the time of this project, students would probably have had limited school experience of data loggers. So in effect, the cohorts of students in the first year were novices to both dataloggers and video analysis. As Jon and Michelle were working within the constraints of an existing programme, all students took one introductory 3-hour datalogging session as this was part of the laboratory programme requirement. They then undertook either the datalogging or video analysis activity.

The cohort of students in that year meant that there were 3 groups (47 students) involved in the video analysis laboratory activity and 11 groups (160 students) in the data logging laboratory activity. The activity cohorts were a random selection but the numbers involved in either activity were a direct consequence of resource availability and time implications.

The students worked in pairs for the video-analysis activity and in groups of threes for the datalogger activity. They worked in pairs for video-analysis in order to reduce crowding around the computers. Resource availability and time implications meant that students worked in threes for the datalogging activity.

The datalogger groups moved objects near an ultrasonic motion datalogger interfaced to a computer and recorded graphs of the motion of these objects. The activity involved the motion of a cart rolling along a bench-top, with and without externally applied forces provided by a person pushing the cart or the pull of a mass hanging from a pulley. The graphs were displayed in real time and students could choose whether to have position, speed or acceleration versus time displayed simultaneously.

The video-analysis groups had exactly the same motions to study, but the objects were on videotape and in the Real-World Physics environment. In effect, the students did not cause the objects to move, but they selected appropriate video-clips and carried out a frame-by-frame analysis using the MotionWorkshop video-analysis tool to investigate the motion of the objects.

Students, as per the norm in these labs, organised themselves within their pairs or groups. They allocated roles and jobs to group members. For example, the datalogging students organised themselves to have a recorder whilst others moved the cart or the mass. In the video-analysis groups, some students manipulated the video excerpts and others tracked the activity on screen or directed progress.

Students began to work on either the video-analysis or datalogging activity about one week after the compulsory datalogging laboratory session. After they had completed the video analysis or datalogging activity, students were invited to volunteer for interviews. Students were interviewed in groups one week after their final laboratory session. Group interviews were used to encourage discussion and trigger student thinking and to try to ensure that students did not construe the interview as a test. The interviews were retrospective. Introspective techniques may have been intrusive and may have influenced student thinking as they engaged with the activity. They might in effect have done things because the interview was forcing them to think about things in a particular way. It is also widely accepted that introspection reduces the student work rate, and there was limited time available for the video-analysis or datalogger laboratory activity. Admittedly, retrospective accounts are recall, rather than thinking at the time, but the interviews do provide us with access to their recall of the way they worked through the activity and the thinking that guided it. It also signals very clearly their sensitivity to aspects of the context and hence their mindfulness or their mindlessness.

The retrospective group interviews were audio taped and transcribed. The transcripts provided in this paper have used the following notation: "-" for interruption and "..." for continuance. The interviewer is represented by "I" and the students have been rendered anonymous through the use of false names.

Findings: Adequacy of Existing Ideas

In this project, several students disregarded the actual experience and/or sequence of information given to them. In some cases, prior knowledge rather than the experimental data determined the sense made of any new experience. Several students said they did not use the activity to challenge the adequacy of their existing ideas. For many of the students, the active presence of past experiences guaranteed the 'correctness' of their practices. This is in keeping with Bourdieu's notion of habitus (Bourdieu, 1992) and Langer's view of mindlessness (Langer, 1993).

During the interviews it rapidly became apparent that students used elements of the video-analysis or the datalogging activity to reinforce these existing ideas, which they accepted as true, rather than question the adequacy of these ideas in light of any conflicting new information. Their existing ideas determined whether students accepted or rejected these new ideas.

Students brought existing ideas to the session and then proceeded to fortify these ideas by drawing on some aspects of the activity that best suited their existing thinking. In effect they started from an assumption that their existing ideas were true. Ali, for example, preferred to use existing knowledge rather than work directly from the experimental data, hence Ali began with the velocity-time graph, whereas in the laboratory session, students encounter the following sequence; position-time, then velocity-time and then acceleration-time graphs. Ali did not like using the information from one graph to construct a second graph, and if Ali has a choice, Ali prefers to start with the velocity time graph. Ali would prefer to use a visualisation strategy to help make sense of the experience. As Ali explained:

> " Because I imagine the ball dropping in my head. I picture it and I think, well, when is the velocity zero and I place that point on my velocity time graph, just to get an indication of everything and where I can join the dots, its much easier for me like that."

This is not to say that Ali did not pay attention, or was not vigilant, because clearly from the above statement, she was. However, she is not mindful, the frame from which she is constructing her new perspective is based on the assumption that her old schema is true, so she is not mindful of the new information.

Some students justified holding on to their preconceived ideas. For example, Jim thought some of the new evidence was problematic rather than instructive:

> "If I didn't know that, say, acceleration didn't have to be in the same direction as velocity then during the prac I probably would have got confused with what was happening ... When I try to describe it I think of $F = ma$. When you push it you have a large force so the large force is overcoming the mg of the weight on the cart and the friction force. So it's overcoming it, and as the friction and mg come into play they slow the ma down because it has no more push in it. I like to visualise it in terms of the actual equations."

Most scientists would accept Jim's view of the direction of acceleration being opposite to the velocity of the object. But he also holds a limited and limiting concept of "push", because for Jim, 'push' is something stored in an object. The fact that he begins by saying – "if I didn't know that..." suggests that he is committed to a rigid belief that stems from an acceptance of information as 'true' without considering that the information he holds may be inaccurate. For Jim there is one predetermined view of the information and he uses the technology to work towards shoring up this predetermined view.

The students working with video-analysis or dataloggers discarded elements of the video-analysis or datalogging exercise that did not compliment their existing framework or their perceived intended outcome. Instead, they used aspects of the datalogging or video-analysis activities to reinforce existing ideas. They ignored the challenge to their thinking and raised the importance of elements that maintained and supported preconceived understandings. Once again, this demonstrates that students are not mindful of the experience they are having.

Findings: Student Goals

Many science concepts taught in school are assumed by many curriculum developers and teachers to be discrete bits of knowledge that are defined formally and depicted in limited examples. For example, Lagowski, (1989) suggests that students perceive chemistry to be symbol manipulation of abstract concepts and hence disembedded thought. Not surprising then that students prepare for their laboratory work by actively preparing for the activity and deciding before conducting the activity, what the appropriate outcomes should be.

The interviews highlighted the fact that students undertake laboratory work with preconceptions firmly embedded and goals already met:

> J: Probably the fact that we spent three hours doing it enforced it more. It really reinforced what I was thinking of and writing out my answers and thinking of it enforced it so um, because say pre-lab when I'm revising for it, I only spend like fifteen to twenty minutes but when you spend three hours on it, it really enforces it in you so you leave the prac and you are almost convinced that you know everything about velocity time graphs and what the distances and areas and all that mean.

The idea of a learner being responsible for their learning in a system that promotes a view of technical rationality has several implications for the learning process. One of these implications is what sense and status the learner affords the new information or learning experience in light of what they already know.

Indeed, as Jim said:

> J: When I try to describe it I think of F=MA. When you push it you have a large force so the large force is overcoming the MG of the weight on the cart and the friction force, so its overcoming it and as the friction and MG come into play, they slow the MA down because its has no more push in it. I like to visualise it in terms of the actual equations and so when it turns around, then okay, so the motion is going that way so the net force is MG+the friction+the force, which equals the force that's going that way.

This type of preparation was further endorsed:

> "That's why before we do pracs we always study the book. We study the book and we read over it and we try and get right in our mind what is happening and what would make sense to happen...."

By encouraging the learning of facts, we have encouraged what Langer (1993) describes as stability seeking. As a consequence, for Jim, the laboratory session did not affect his incorrect concept that the weight acting vertically affects the horizontal motion. Jim was not guided by an inherent interest in the activity, instead he was trying to discern the tangible outcomes as required by the course. The extent of commitment and purpose is determined by his perception of the required outcomes. This in itself is not an issue, providing it does not become the sole focus of a learning activity. If it does, it will limit the value of the situation as an appropriate context and render the students' actions and practices within the situation purposeless for the individual student. As a purposeless activity, the concepts hold little intrinsic meaning and the students end up making limited if any links to appropriate contexts, or new experiences. It is even less surprising then to find that students hold on to their established ideas and find ways to compound their existing position, even when the evidence from a new experience/activity does not support their existing view.

In many instances laboratory activity provides opportunities for students to demonstrate achievement in solving mathematical problems. This is not necessarily indicative of their understanding of a science concept. Many activity questions encourage students to recall definitions or apply computational skills and many of the interviewed students, conscious of these requirements, attended to their laboratory work accordingly regardless of the ICT used, or the manner in which the ICT was challenging their inaccurate views. Indeed, I would suggest that in this case, the focus on achievement seems to inadvertently compound misconceptions, even when there is scope to challenge student thinking.

Findings: Situation in which the Learning Occurs

Kinaesthetic elements of both tasks were used by students to help make sense of their data. The following is an excerpt taken from the interview with a group of students.

I: Okay. Which aspect of that task do you think helped you with your understanding about -

J: Interpreting what the graph was doing, so um, pushing it along we sort of, we can get an idea it went faster than slower with the friction and just interpreting what the graph was doing with what we had actually done with the trolley was good I thought.

I: I'm afraid I don't quite understand that. What do you mean interpreting?

J: Well, because we had to copy the graph down so to do that we had to really have a look at the graph and understand what it was doing. Because it was just lines going everywhere and we had to understand what was happening.

I: Like, for example -

J: - Okay, say we pushed the trolley along and we went fast to begin and then went slowly because of friction got slower and we could say a velocity graph we could see it was sloped down so we can understand what was happening.

I: So did you keep your hand pushing on the trolley?

J: We just pushed it, well whatever we had to do. Sometimes you had to keep a constant force so there was no acceleration and just pushed along or um, it was like push or whatever.

I: Is that what you did as well M?

M: Yeah, it just said in the book like First Year had to sort of, not in this order, but you had to push it all the way with your hand or you just had to give it a push and then it would go off by itself and you'd see what happened. And you had sometimes graphs like views and you had to say at the highest point what the cart was doing and at the middle where it crossed the axis what the cart was doing and at the bottom what the cart was doing, so that's what we were doing by interpreting the graph.

I: What elements of that whole time do you think helped you with your ideas about motion?

M: Well, I like the idea of it better than a video because I like to do things myself and because I am actually doing it I understand it better - what I'm doing -

I: - What do you mean "doing"?

M: Pushing the cart - you know, I'm sort of in control of it so I can see and then I can interpret the graph from that - whereas if I just saw a graph from a video, I mean it just wouldn't have the same impact because I didn't "do" it, I'm just looking at it sort of thing.

The 'hands-on' interaction in the datalogging activity, for example students pushing the cart and observing the graph produced as they pushed the cart appeared to encourage their understanding of the construction of graphs. As Xena said:

> "Moving objects allowed me to see what different movements would do to the graphs. Controlling the object helped me to understand how graphs were formed."

This is a commonly perceived advantage of dataloggers. Indeed, one of the most often cited datalogging motion activities involving an ultrasound motion sensor requires students to move in front of the motion sensor in order to try to recreate the position time graph depicted on the computer screen. The user has to interpret the position-time pattern and mimic the pattern observed on screen by moving in front of the ultrasound sensor. Anecdotal evidence would suggest that this strategy is successful in helping students interpret graphs and engage in what Dewey might call active learning, or what Langer (1993) calls mindful learning. It could be argued that the physical manipulation of the cart and the resulting on-screen graph may encourage mindfulness.

The video-analysis activity also gave some students a degree of active engagement and mindfulness. The video analysis of the ball bouncing meant that students could slow the action and in doing this, they could track and interpret the ball's movement in terms of the developing in situ graph. As Ali explained, the opportunity to slow the action provided her with scope to interpret the concept that was being illustrated:

> " Like you get to see it all - it would normally go really quickly, but because it sort of freezes at all these time intervals you sort of get to see it spread out - its motion and the velocity"

Therefore, viewing graphs in synchronisation with the action of either the ball or cart, or against the construction of other graphs, helped some students interpret the ideas and consequently we could argue that they were engaged in mindful activity. The activity provided them with an opportunity to actively focus on the material in front of them and in so doing negotiate what they were doing in light of what they knew and were learning.

The capacity of video-analysis to provide opportunity to view several graphs was another influential factor. This provided students with an opportunity to identify and compare the relationships between patterns. In working with three screen shots in tandem, Claire was able to try to negotiate meaning for new ideas, and old ideas, this again could be considered mindful behaviour.

As Claire explained:

> " On the computer you could go to like a part of the program where you had the distance versus time graph, then the velocity versus time graph and the acceleration versus time graph underneath each other."

An unfortunate side effect of working with the computers was the fact that some students assumed the video-analysis was more accurate and being mindful of this new information, as well as being unaware of this perception, may lead students to hold onto inaccurate ideas. Students assumed that the computer was 'perfect' and computer presented information was infallible and accurate so, for example, they did not take into account the skill of the person in the video clip.

Any support perceived to be delivered by something that has no error (such as the computer) may result in already problematic conceptual understanding being further reinforced. This could result in future dependent or related concepts being influenced by incorrect deductions and understanding.

DISCUSSION

Donaldson (1993) wrote "passionate curiosity empowers the intellect", yet much of the evidence provided in this chapter indicates that many students have a limited curiosity when engaged in practical work at this level. This may be due to their conditioning toward the outcome based nature of most practical work.

The project findings would suggest that more notice should be taken of the notion of assessment and the design of appropriate laboratory activity. With the push to include ICT in more science courses there comes an associated need to ensure the activities are well scaffolded and the nature of assessment needs to be changed accordingly. Some of the students' comments would suggest that science educators at tertiary institutions should reconsider their conceptual-teaching pedagogy and related assessment. Dwelling on learning achievement in the form of outcomes may provide us with a misleading perspective of students' understanding of the concepts. If we only monitor achievement or outcomes, we will fail to promote learning and fail to support students' acquisition of an understanding that enables them to address and comprehend other related concepts.

In using video-analysis or dataloggers without the process of social interaction, involving those who are familiar with more accurate views of the concepts, the student's incorrect constructs will probably continue to be upheld if they engage in mindless activity with computers. To a certain extent if the students' views are in accord with scientific views, then the process of social interaction has limited need, as the views held would not be problematic in the long term. Indeed, the independent fortification of their ideas through the use of ICT could be useful and would have little or limited negative consequence in the development of other concepts. Concern arises when ideas are inappropriate and students are not mindful, that is they do not take into account the experience, but hold onto their existing ideas, even if these are in conflict with new events.

Laboratory activity involving the use of ICT should require students to make their thinking visible as well as require documentation of their final result. Their ideas can then be discussed and challenged or supported. The use of dataloggers, and simulations in themselves do not include or foster these facilities, and it is therefore important for the facilitator to access the processes students use and to encourage mindful rather than mindless activity. The inclusion of reflective challenges and applications in an activity associated with video-analysis or dataloggers may help students consider the adequacy of their ideas. Giving equal weighting to the process as well as the outcome may enable students to reflect on and accommodate key concepts.

The nature and mechanism for mindful engagement clearly does affect the students' ability to access the science. If learning is to be enhanced, the technology needs to be more than a tool through which we continue to use didactic practices as this will simply serve to encourage students to commit to already held rigid beliefs and to engage in mindless activity. Immersing students in an ICT rich learning environment may provide opportunities for success if the interaction between students and facilitators allow for prior, usually robust, learning beliefs to be reviewed and discussed and if the students are encouraged to engage in mindful activity. We should not simply be advocating that students simply learn scientific facts, we should be encouraging them to interpret these facts or at least view them as interpretable.

Simply relying on the ICT to challenge thinking may only serve to reinforce existing concepts and thinking. The project highlights the crucial nature of learning activities and the critical importance of designing carefully researched activities if we are to expect students to engage mindfully with the technology. Without appropriate task designs, either within the software or within the activity, the intended learning experience may be significantly different to the experienced learning, as students may engage in mindless, rather than mindful activity. The difference between the learning experience and the experienced learning may not simply be a consequence of the students' cognitive ability, nor the forced use of various ICT. It may be a consequence of thinking dispositions in terms of behavioural tendencies, mindfulness and fruitfulness.

Behavioural tendencies are different to the students' capabilities, in that students have to have more than cognitive ability, they have to be disposed toward investing some mental effort in terms of exploration, organisation and intellectual risk. Our current use of ICT focuses very strongly on students' abilities in terms of skill acquisition, rather than their thinking disposition toward the use of ICT in a more alert and thoughtful way. Nor surprisingly then, students come to use the ICT to simply reinforce what they already know, rather than view what they know from a different perspective.

A mindful student will engage with a situation in such a way as to allow the use of strategies to reconstruct their perspective. In using ICT we need to encourage students to develop habits of mind that result in the technology being used to do more than compound existing ideas. This requires fostering a disposition toward being open minded and managing activities in an alert and thoughtful way, rather than being disposed toward constancy. For most students constancy is the main goal, because we have fostered a culture of learning science as the learning of 'fact'. Most educators present students with information (facts) with little regard as to the relevance of this information to the student beyond the need to know it for assessment purposes. Most students have determined this purpose and work steadily toward achieving it. The result is that students have no reason to engage in mindfulness. Nor do they have to confront and challenge their ideas which are already embedded.

Once the learner is locked into a given version of information they will find it difficult to reconsider what they have accepted as true because the new information has limited usefulness, and is not any more fruitful to them. They are committed, albeit, in some cases prematurely to a view that has served them well in the past and afforded them recognised progress and attainment. After all, if the students' rigid views match the information base of those conducting the assessment, then we judge these students to be intelligent. Several of the students in this study processed the information made available through the use of dataloggers and video analysis in what Langer (1993) would call a mindless way. They did not reconsider their views on the information garnered through the use of the ICT because they had no reason to think about it and have been encouraged to adopt what Langer (1993) describes as premature cognitive commitment. That is, the students hold rigid beliefs which result in mindless acceptance of information without the consideration of alternative views of that information. This is a pity, as the potential of the technology lies in its ability to provide information from a different perspective and we, as educators should be striving to encourage students to view information from a range of perspectives.

Most science educators would agree that if practical work involving ICT fails to help students learn science, learn about science or do science, then the ICT should not be used. It has been argued that certain ICT would simplify the complexity and routine of science (see for example, NCET, nd, Rogers 1990; Scaife 1993. This however is inconsequential if students are not disposed toward working with the ICT in a mindful way and if we continue to promote learning science as a technical rationalist process, in which students routinely follow established rules and practices in order to make progress. We currently deploy mechanisms which document learner achievement without encouraging learners to take some responsibility for being critical, self regulating, comprehensive and autonomous learners. So how then can we expect them to make mindful use of powerful ICT? Perhaps we should start by encouraging the development of dispositions toward reflexive engagement.

REFERENCES

Beichner, R. J. (1990) The effect of simultaneous motion presentation and graph generation in a kinematics lab, *The Physics Teacher,* 27, pp. 803-815.

Bourdieu, P. (1992) *An Invitation to Reflexive Sociology.* Cambridge Polity Press.

Brungardt, J. B & Zollamnda, D. A. (1996) The influence of interactive video disc instruction using real time analysis on kinematics graphing skills of high school physics students. *Journal of Research in Science Teaching*, 32 pp. 855-869.

Chinn, C. A & Brewer, W.F (1993) The role of anomalous data in knowledge acquisition: a theoretical framework and implications for science instruction. *Review of Educational Research,* 63, pp. 3-49

Coleman, M (1996) The software scene in science. *Education in Science*, 167, pp. 8-10

Donaldson, Margaret (1993) *Human minds: an exploration.* New York: Allen Lane/Penguin

Education. *Educational Pyschologist*, 28 (1) pp. 67-85

Escalada, L.T. & Zollman, D. (1996) An Investigation on the Effects of Using Interactive Video in a Physics Classroom on Student Learning and Attitudes. *Journal of Research in ScienceTeaching* 34, pp. 476-489.

Fiske, S.T and Taylor, S. E (1984) Social cognition. New York: Random House.

Harwood, W. S. & McMahon, M. M. (1997) Effects of integrated video media on student achievement and attitudes in High School Chemistry. *Journal of Research in Science Teaching,* 34, 6, pp. 17-631.

Hodson, D (1996). Laboratory work as scientific method: three decades of confusion and distortion' *J.Curriculum Studies*, 28, (2), pp. 115- 135

Hodson, D. (1992). Assessment of practical work; some considerations in philosophy of science. *Science and Education*, 1, pp. 115-44

Hodson, D.. (1998) Taking practical work beyond the laboratory. Guest Editorial, *International Journal of Science Education*, 20,6, pp. 629-632.

Kinzie,M. B., Strauss, R., and Foss, J (1993) The effects of an interactive dissection simulation on the performance and attitudes of high school biology students. *Journal of Research in Science Teaching*, 30, 8 pp. 989 - 1000.

Kirschner, P. & Huisman, W. (1998) Dry laboratories in science education: computer-based practical work, *International Journal of Science Education, 20,* 6, pp. 665-682.

Korthagen, F and Lagerwerf, B (1995) levels in Learning. Journal of Research in Science Teaching, 32, 10 p 1011-1038

Lagowski, J. J. (Ed.).(1989)   Editorial notes. Chemistry; tool or discipline? Journal of Chemical Education, 66 (9), September p 701.

Langer, E.J (1993) A Mindful Education. *Educational Pyschologist*, 28 (1) pp. 43-50

Linn, M and Songer, N. B (1991) How do students' views of science influence knowledge integration? *Journal of Research in Science Teaching*, 28, 9 pp. 761 -784

Merleau-Ponty, Maurice (1962) *Phenomenology of Perception,* London: Routledge and Kegan Paul

Mingers, John (1995) *Self-Producing Systems: Implications and Applications of Autopoiesis,* New York: Plenum Press

Newton, L (1997) Graph talk; Some observations and reflections on students' datalogging. *School Science Review*, 79, 287, pp. 49-54

Osborne, R. & Wittrock, M. (1985) The generative learning model and its implications for science education. *Studies in Science Education,* 12, pp. 59-87.

Pearce, J. M. (1988) Measuring Speed Using a Computer: Several Techniques. *Physics Education*, 23, pp. 291-296.

Pearce, J. M. (1993) Measuring Motion Using a Macintosh Computer, Australian. *Science Teachers Journal*, 39, 2, pp. 44-51.

Pearce, J.M. & Livett, M.K. (1997) Real-World Physics: a Java-based Web Environment for the Study of Physics, Proceedings of AusWeb97, Brisbane, (July 1997) CDROM.

Perkins, D., Jay, E., Tishman, S. (1993) New Conceptions of thinking: From Ontology to

Redish, E.F., Saul, J.M. & Steinburg ,R.N. (1997) On the Effectiveness of Active-Engagement Microcomputer-Based Laboratories. *American Journal of Physics*, 65, pp. 45- 54.

Rodrigues, S. (1997) The role of information technology in secondary school science: an illustrative review. *School Science Review* 79, 287, pp. 35-40.

Rodrigues, S, Pearce, J and Livett, M (2001) Using Video-Analysis or Data loggers During Practical work in first year physics, Educational Studies, 27,1,31-44.

Rogers, L. (1990) IT in the Science National Curriculum.

Rogers, L. T (1995) The computer as an aid for exploring graphs. *School Science Review*, 76, 276, pp. 31-39

Scaife, J (1993) Datalogging: Where are we now? *Physics education*, 28, pp. 83 - 86

Scanlon, E., O'Shea, T., Smith, R., Taylor, J. & O'Malley, C. (1993) Running in the rain: using a shared simulation to solve open ended physics problems. *Physics education* 28, pp.107-113.

Steed, M. (1992) STELLA, A simulation construction kit: Cognitive process and educational implications, *Journal of Computers in Mathematics and Science Teaching*, 11, pp. 39 –52.

Summers, M, Solomon, J, Bevan, R, Frost, A, Reynolds, H, Zimmerman, C (1991) Can pupils learn through their own movement? A study of the use of a motion sensor interface. *Physics Education*, 26, 6, pp. 345 -349

White, R. T. (1992) Implications of recent research on learning for curriculum and assessment. Journal of Curriculum Studies, 24 (2), p 153 -164.

STUDENT DISPOSITION TOWARD AUTONOMY AND FACETS OF CHEMISTRY CDROMS

Susan Rodrigues

INTRODUCTION

For me, there are a few key questions we should be asking ourselves when we promote the use of Information Communication Technologies (ICT) in classrooms:

Does it make a difference?
How does it make a difference?
What is the value of this difference?

One of the anticipated differences is the opportunity to develop the learner's own initiative. Indeed, to a certain extent we promote the notion of learner centred pedagogy which promotes learner choice, a degree of autonomy and the acquisition and development of generic skills associated with learner managed learning. Yet there is a dearth of documentation on the impact of ICT in terms of the development of learner's initiatives in scientific discovery learning (De Jong and Van Joolingen, 1998). Wu, Krajcik and Soloway (2001) suggest there is limited research documenting how students develop chemistry representational skills or identify the interaction between the visual and conceptual aspects of chemical representations..

Non-linear access to large stores of information (Nielsen, 1995), learners developing self directed learning strategies (De Jong and Van Joolingen, 1998), the opportunity for user initiative and self pace (Barrett, 1988) and the promotion of engagement and motivation (Jonassen, 1989) have all been cited as reasons to use ICT in classrooms. All of these arguments have user ownership at their core. Non linear access does not reside in the technology; it depends on the user to explore the technology in a non-linear way. Therefore self-pace and user initiative does not reside in the technology, it is user dependent. Users' dispositions towards use of the technology are therefore critical factors in the use of the available technology to enhance their learning. So, for me, to what extent ICT encourages or requires learner autonomy or the development of learner initiative requires further investigation and documentation. The studies that are reported in this chapter were designed to identify patterns of learner initiative when using ICT.

The promotion of user-centred interactive environments is possibly one of the key incentives for the use of CDROMS in classroom, because they have the potential to encourage students to be pro-active learners (McCarthy 1989) in a self-pacing and non-threatening environment. Indeed as Ainley and Pearce report in the final chapter, other studies have suggested that increased level of interactivity results in improved learning and better attitudes toward learning. I am interested in the extent to which students' dispositions influence their use of CDROMS, and hence potentially the effectiveness of CDROMS in teaching and learning. I am interested in the manner in which students access information from CDROMS when given free access and open task direction.

In this chapter I am going to report on findings from two projects, in order to help illustrate how animations of microscopic interpretations of macroscopic events or video of macroscopic events, influence pupils' understanding of, and dispositions toward, learning about science. I am going to refer to the first project as the Periodic CDROM project and the second project as the Video/Animation project.

SOME OF THE RATIONALE FOR THE PROJECTS

The last few decades have seen a significant change in the nature of educational material offered through various multimedia systems (Dillon and Gabbard, 1998). The CDROM is more available and affordable and is being widely promoted for use in schools. Not a day goes by without a CDROM on some science topic or other appearing on my desk for perusal, comment or formal review. Most of the CDROMS are well presented, include high quality graphics, look very professional and seem to contain information on school relevant science. When I view them I always wonder whether they will make a difference to students' learning. In what way will the various components affect the way students use the CDROM? To what extent will the students take responsibility for becoming comprehensive CDROM reviewers? To what extent will they use the various facets to support their learning? Basically I question student disposition toward autonomy and interaction involving Chemistry CDROMS. This is not because I want to belittle the value of many ICT initiatives, but because I want to look at the persuasive argument for learner management of learning and ask what are some of the factors that influence the self-managing learner.

My investigation sought to observe learner interaction with facets of CDROMS that are increasingly common within Chemistry CDROMS. I am particularly interested in what happens when the user has responsibility for their choice, action and direction. I am interested in this aspect because while I favour the Constructivist view of learning, I believe that inadequate attention has been paid to the impact of students' dispositions towards autonomy when attempting to encourage assimilation and accommodation of knowledge. While there is evidence to show that prior experiences influence learning and there is evidence to show that the relevance of the experience affects their learning, there is limited documentation on students' dispositions toward taking ownership for their learning.

With the onset of computer use in classrooms, learner-computer dialogue is crucial, but it is equally important for at least one of the parties engaged in this dialogue to have an intrinsic incentive to interact and engage in dialogue. While a computer has been programmed to respond, its partner in the dialogue has the responsibility for initiative. Therefore there is even more reason to consider learner disposition toward learning, if computer use is expecting learners to show initiative and be favourably disposed towards demonstrating initiative.

In this chapter I do not engage in a discussion on ICT – human dialogue. A discussion on the nature of interactivity can be found in the chapter by Ainley and Pearce. My focus in this chapter is mainly on disposition toward autonomy. It is my contention that we need to consider student disposition toward working independently within an ICT environment. The ICT environment I have chosen to focus on is that of the use of Chemistry CDROMs in classrooms. I begin with an exploration of particular views of learning and then provide a brief review on why Chemistry CDROMs are advocated for classroom use.

Some Views on Learning

Constructvist views, of which there are many forms, for example, Personal Constructivism (see Hodson and Hodson, 1998), Radical Constructivism (von Glaserfeld, 1989), Social Constructivism (Vygotsky, 1987), have gone some way toward explaining why the delivery of information does not result in understanding. Though the variety of terms may cause confusion, they all commonly perceive learning to be the reconstruction rather than delivery of knowledge. Constructivism is one possible lens through which to view learning. When viewed through this lens, social endeavour and the situatedness of learning are crucial elements in the promotion of learning.

The characterisation of learning as a social endeavour is also consistent with Symbolic interactionist schools of thought. Symbolic interactionists (Blumer, 1969) suggest that individuals act according to the meanings that they attribute to their experiences. In effect, meanings are deemed to be constructed and modified through social interaction processes. However, Symbolic interactionists see learning as more than solely founded on meanings attributed to knowledge or what the learning process entails, they recognise the impact of context and experience on dispositions toward learning. If we view disposition as an orientation to the practise of learning, then disposition links meaning, participation and action.

A View on Disposition

It has been suggested that curriculum development needs to look at goals related to knowledge, skills, dispositions and feelings (Katz, 1993). Most educators would concede knowledge and skill acquisition is a given education goal, and many would also concede that self esteem and affective nuances influence the learning experience. However, while attitudes are often cited as goals, the influence of disposition is seldom made explicit. Perkins, Jay and Tishman (1993, p75) define dispositions as "people's tendencies to put their capabilities into action." The Symbolic interactionist view of learning would suggest that disposition has a significant impact on students attending to particular aspects of their learning. Bourdieu (1992) talks about *habitus*; a portfolio of dispositions to all aspects of life. This portfolio of dispositions is usually tacit but it has significant influence on any given action in a particular situation. Dispositions to learning are founded on the meanings that individuals attribute to what knowledge is and the learning process itself. Bourdieu's *habitus* shares some ideology with a view promoted by symbolic interactionists, such as Blumer (1969, 74) who suggested that actions are constructed through a process of social interaction 'by actors out of what they take into account'.

Katz (1993) defines disposition as a tendency to voluntarily, frequently and intentionally exhibit patterns of behaviour that are directed towards a particular goal. For example, curiosity is a disposition and those who are curious, explore, examine and question their environment. It should be noted that there is a significant difference in having a disposition to be a comic and having the skills needed for comedy. But someone who has the skills will not necessarily be a comic if they are not disposed in that way. Mindfulness, as proposed by Langer (1993) may be viewed as a disposition because it refers to how disposed the learner is toward considering and processing information in a flexible and alert way. Disposition should be viewed as akin to, but distinct from, motivation, and whilst there is abundant literature on student motivation to use ICT, there is only inferred documentation regarding the influence of disposition on their use of ICT.

We should be considering the impact of disposition in light of the growing inclusion of ICT for autonomous classroom practice. As Perkins, Jay and Tishman (1993) suggest, good thinkers are not differentiated from average thinkers simply through better cognitive ability, what often differentiates thinkers is their thinking disposition.

In addition if we have a view that the teaching process through which knowledge and skills are promoted may affect the learner's disposition then we, as educators, should explore the nature and impact of these dispositions as well as the process used. For just as drill and practice reading routines may actually undermine the learners reading disposition (Katz, 1993), likewise various facets commonly found in Chemistry CDROMS may undermine students' dispositions toward using them to learn chemistry. As Cantor (1990) suggests, 'having' does not automatically result in 'doing'.

CDROMS and Teaching and Learning

Many students find learning chemistry confusing (Herron and Greenbowe, 1986). Not surprising really, as we expect students to become familiar with the microscopic (particles), macroscopic (everyday substances), and symbolic (formula and equation) aspects of chemistry (Johnstone, 1993) and then establish relationships between, and work interchangeably with, these representations. For example students observe melting at a macroscopic level (ice melting to form liquid water), they account for these observations through interpretation at the microscopic level (weak bonds between molecules are broken) and they are expected to provide algebraic type annotations using predetermined symbols to report on these observations ($H_2O_{(s)}$ → $H_2O_{(l)}$. Their ability to operate with the macroscopic, microscopic and symbolic levels is taken to be an indication of their understanding of the chemistry. There is a hope that the currently available technology can help make these links more meaningful for students. According to Harwood and McMahon (1997) user centred interactive environments could encourage students to become pro-active learners.

There is a growing body of literature advocating, describing or evaluating classroom practice that stresses the learner's own initiative, through the use of the ICT. However, for the most part, new ICT is often employed within didactic teaching models, where knowledge is seen as facts and teaching perceived to be the delivery of these facts. Hence, to a certain extent the ICT introduced into the classroom has not changed classroom practice just changed the nature of the tool used to deliver information. Much like using pen and paper instead of chalk and slate; the manner in which they are used does not change, and what is taught does not change, but the tools change.

Kozma, (1994) has suggested that successful learning involves the reconstruction of the real world by the learner and the use of ICT has the potential to assist in this reconstruction. Aitkins (1993) suggests that motivation and interest in the learning task increase when the learner is cast in an active role. However, Fideris (1988) suggests that learner control is not necessarily automatic and some learners may not simply require access, they may require guidance. Never the less, CD ROMS have the potential to place the learner at the centre of control. As Park and Hannafin (1993, p63) suggest:

> Interactive multimedia dynamically link and manage nodes of information containing multiple symbol systems and images within a given medium or across different media. ...they provide user directed, non-linear methods for organising and accessing information...support access to knowledge according to individual demands...and provide a user-centred interactive environment.

Therefore a user has the opportunity to decide on direction and purpose.

The impact of CDROMS on learner control, the development of learning strategies and concept reconstruction are all crucial in terms of meeting

Constructivist tenets and it has been argued that these types of technologies encourage concept development (Kearsley 1988). Costanzo (1988) goes so far as to say they promote interconnectedness of knowledge. CDROMS are three-dimensional concept and process webs that offer students non-linear access to information. Marchionini (1988) suggests that they influence different learning strategies. This may be because CDROMS provide an opportunity for students to review, elaborate on, and summarise data during the process of conceptual reconstruction. Trotter (1989) indicates the potential of ICT to foster learner control. As CDROMS are multimedia, they provide what Marchionini (1988, p9) calls:

> A fluid environment requiring learners to constantly make decisions, and evaluate progress, thus forcing the students to apply higher order thinking skills.

In light of these strengths, CDROMS clearly address the ideology promoted by Constructivist school of thought.

While we are still not sure how individuals encode their representations, people like Gardner (1993) have suggested that knowledge can be represented in different ways. Much research has described how students could be helped to develop conceptual understanding of Chemical representations, and much of this relies on an assertion that students need to actively construct their knowledge. The deployment of CDROMS is thought to assist in this process in chemistry because CDROMS are thought to help students visualise the links between the macroscopic, microscopic and symbolic facets of school science. Wu, Krajcik and Soloway, (2001) have argued that when students understand representations they can generate interpretations and manipulate the representations. It may even be the case that multiple linked representations encourage students to understand abstract chemical ideas.

Many educators and designers include video or animation clips in CDROMS in an attempt to make the science representation more holistic, more representative and more accurate. Textbooks provide symbolic notation and descriptions or static presentations of the microscopic and macroscopic but multimedia has the potential, through animations and video clips, to make the microscopic level in chemistry more explicit and related to the macroscopic and symbolic. Though it should be stated that the jury is still out with respect to the effectiveness of video as a medium to support student learning as compared with real, hands-on laboratory experiences. I do not intend to engage in that particular debate, but discussions on using microcomputer-based and video-based resources can be found in Beichner (1990) and Escalada & Zollman (1996).

A real challenge to learning chemistry is that chemistry involves the use of minute particles to represent macroscopic changes. Reactions at particle level are difficult to explain and visualise when we teach classroom chemistry. For example, I remember a student telling me that the colour change for a titration involving potassium permanganate (where the solution changes from an aubergine colour to a pale pink) was a dilution effect, much like the dilution of concentrated orange juice. Unfortunately it was my role as a chemistry teacher to convince him that it was actually a change in oxidation states and represented the formation of new ions.

Chemistry teachers use models to help explain chemical reactions at particulate level. Four common models used in chemistry classrooms are: space filling models, ball and stick models, Lewis structure (electron dot) models and formula models (line drawing representations). The visual representation of complicated reactions or changes at particulate level is fraught with difficulty. For example, how does one use ball and stick models to illustrate sublimation of iodine?

CD-ROMS often use animation to 'revisualise' static space filling or ball and stick models of molecules. Many chemistry CD-ROMs provide animated molecular models and video clips of laboratory experiments as well as animated simulations to depict abstract particle chemistry (Brooks and Brooks, 1996). These animated models are thought to provide a graphic depiction of molecular models for macroscopic phenomena. But Anderson (1990) suggests that many students think the properties depicted at the animated microscopic level represent the properties at the macroscopic level. As a result, students who have viewed an animation involving coloured particles may argue that individual particles are indeed coloured. This concern has been voiced previously, with respect to the use of other models. It could be argued that students think that coloured ball and stick concrete models are indicative of the colour of the atom. In my opinion, most students see the ball and stick concrete model as a representation rather than reality, whereas most computer simulated information is perceived by students to be reality, probably because much computer generated science imagery is talked about and promoted as reality. We have yet to 'see' an atom, but we do have the technology to simulate their 'appearance', and accept these as snapshots of 'atoms'. The use of increasingly hi-tech CDROM animations for molecules may result in the same type of acceptance, where simulated behaviours and appearances have the potential to influence student constructs of those abstract concepts. This may or may not be problematic, as it has been argued that a learner can form better mental models when presented with dynamic visual information instead of static information (Cognition and Technology Group, 1991).

I would argue that involving CDROMS in the learning of chemistry should include developing a disposition toward CDROMS that enable the user to become autonomous comprehensive learners. Students' multimedia related dispositions are manifested in their confidence, their interest, their perseverance and their ability to think about their thinking. CDROMs designed specifically for classroom use, either as textbooks, databases, simulations or tutorial packages, typically contain video clips and/or animations with accompanying text. This chapter discusses findings stemming from two projects that investigated student disposition toward these types of features commonly found in Chemistry CDROMS. A key question was to what extent does disposition that is the students' orientation to the practice of learning, impact on student progress?

OVERVIEW OF THE PRODUCTS USED IN THE TWO PROJECTS

The Periodic CDROM project investigated a CDROM that included simulations, graphics, video clips of experiments, notes and images on the topic of Elements in the Periodic table. The Periodic CDROM took on board many of the criteria noted by Mayer (2001) as specifics that support learning. For example it provided text and graphics, kept analogous words close on the screen, presented analogous words and pictures simultaneously instead of successively, and provided animation and narration, or animation and text. If used systematically, the Periodic CDROM increased the level of difficulty in terms of conceptual understanding required for the abstract ideas and it presented a degree of structure that could allow for scaffolded progression.

The main menu of the Periodic CDROM has four sections: Atomic Structure, Periodic Table, Quiz and Help. The CDROM is a well-resourced environment in which there is quality data, in the form of graphics, animations, video and sound segments reflecting key aspects of atomic structure and periodicity. There is also an on-line help device that enables the user to access prompt messages when they are unsure about functions or features of particular objects on the screen. The Atomic Structure section has six sub units on atoms, atom building, radioactive Decay, Isotopes, Decay series and Half-life. The periodic table section allows students to access detail relating uses, properties and histories for various elements in the periodic table. The quiz section has three options, a 90-second quiz, a 5-minute quiz and a sudden death quiz. The Help section is an information section that provides the user with an overview of what is available on the disc.

The second project involved an investigation into the video/animation facet commonly found in CDROMS. It employed a custom designed package that tracked students' engagement. Mary Ainley brought the technique employed in this project to my attention. She had used it in other research studies (See Ainley, Hidi, & Tran, 1997). The technique involved using a custom-designed software package called Between the Lines modified to include animation and video clips in order to suit the purposes of the CDROM project.

The modified Between the Lines package included animation and video clips, with or without accompanying text, on the topics of dissolving, melting and boiling. The video clips of macroscopic events included water boiling in a kettle, water forming steam, ice melting in a cup, a heated glass rod being drawn out, sugar stirred into colourless water, and orange granules stirred into colourless water (see for example figure1).

Figure 1

The animation clips were based on 3D molecular models of molecules of water changing state (see figure 2) or other 3D models of substances such as salt being added to the molecular models of liquid water.

Figure 2

The Between the Lines package tracked the students' access and use of the various segments. Students also completed brief questionnaires and were observed using the software.

Relying solely on attitude questionnaires to access information on student disposition would not have been fruitful, because the questionnaires would be unlikely to capture the portfolio of interlinked perceptions, beliefs and values that scaffold student disposition. A key focus for the research was the students' disposition toward presentation mode in terms of utility and functionality. I was interested in how different multimedia features commonly found in CDROMS influence student disposition toward use of these facets. Observation of student participation provides a window into student disposition that can be explored through the use of open-ended questions. The nature and degree of the 'observation' within each project was different, hence in the next couple of sections I provide more information about each project.

DETAILS OF THE PERIODIC CDROM PROJECT

The Periodic CDROM project involved one class who took part in the study because the topic was due to be studied at that time and their Head of Science was interested in the use of CDROMS for chemistry. The teacher and class volunteered to take part. It was agreed that pairs of students would use the Periodic CDROM for 20 minutes during the course of each chemistry lesson on the topic. In a usual one-hour lesson, six students had access to the CDROM that was housed in the room next door. Twenty female year ten, (14 -15 year old) students worked in pairs with the Periodic CDROM. The female students were above average ability but had no school based experiences related to using interactive CDROMS. Hence these students could be termed 'novices' however, from observation it was apparent that the majority of these students had a basic familiarity with CDROMS, gained in other environments. Each student was told to simply use the CDROM to learn about the Periodic table.

The data was collected through the use of pre- and post- questionnaires and videotaped observations of the pairs of students working with the CDROM. Researcher notes supplemented the videotapes and the tapes were later subjected to detailed visual analysis aimed at establishing the nature of the behaviour and interactions every five seconds when students worked with the CDROM.

The pre- and post-questionnaires helped to determine the students' dispositions towards learning with multimedia programs. Both the pre and post questionnaires contained the same twenty attitude items and included a number of test questions on the concepts of atomic structure and periodicity. The attitude item statements employed in both questionnaires were derived from previously validated instruments (Francis, 1993; Shashaani, 1993; Robertson et al., 1995). The attitude items measured four categories: interest in learning with CDROMS, confidence in using CDROMS, concepts of CDROMS and personal preference with respect to instruction methods. The pre-project questionnaire was administered during class time, three weeks prior to the students using the CDROM and the post-project questionnaire was completed one week after all the students had used the CDROM.

The Video/Animation CDROM Project

The video/animation CDROM project investigated presentation mode in terms of utilisation and usefulness when learning about boiling, melting and dissolving at a level identified as appropriate within the school syllabus for 11-13 year old students. There were 11 male and 11 female students aged between 11 and 13, who had varying degrees of interest and ability in science.

Most people have watched numerous ice cubes melt and I doubted whether pupils would be riveted watching a video clip of an ice cube melt, however this enabled me to propose that pupil choice of these clips wasn't simply the content, but the whole context, which included the presentation mechanism. I could have created animations to represent boiling water from a macroscopic level. I wasn't interested in this aspect, as most Chemistry CDROM animations tend to provide animations of events from the microscopic angle while video clips tend to provide the macroscopic event and I was interested in investigating the currently available material that is advocated for school use.

Students were coded to match survey responses to their computer log on the Between the Lines package. The computer recorded students' ages, gender and general interests before allowing students to complete practice screens to familiarise themselves with the scales used to measure their stated interest levels and the screens. The students did not know which mini topic (ie dissolving sugar in water or dissolving orange crystals in water) would be viewed in the mode they selected.

The computer log also recorded students' preferences for teaching/learning strategies such as learning on their own, learning with a computer, learning with a group, or learning with a teacher.

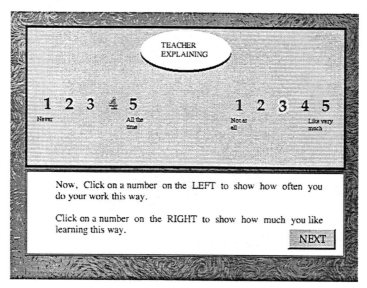

Figure 3. Screen shot asking about student's preferences for teaching styles

Students then viewed four compulsory examples of the different multimedia presentations. This was to familiarise them with all four presentation styles and put them in an informed position to choose a preferred presentation type when learning about melting, boiling and dissolving.

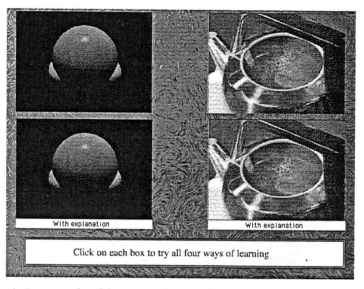

Figure 4. An example of the screen shot for the four presentation types available.

Basically the four presentation types were:

- 3D molecular model animations at microscopic level
- 3D molecular model animations at microscopic level with explanatory text
- video clip example at macroscopic level
- video clip example at macroscopic level and explanatory text

Students were asked to rate their interest in the melting, boiling and dissolving topics.

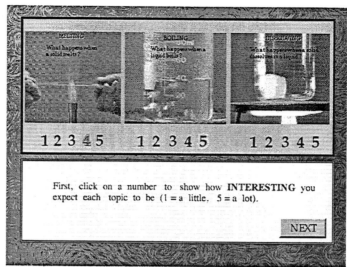

Figure 5 Examples of the video clips for the three topics

They then faced another screen that asked them to select the topics and presentation style to start. After one topic students could opt to view another screen on the same topic or select a new topic. If they opted for a new topic, they had to complete multiple-choice chemistry questions before the computer gave them access to the next topic. Their responses to the multiple-choice questions were logged as part of the record. If they opted to view another screen on the same topic, they had four presentation styles to choose from. The computer programme logged students' choices and responses as they worked through the programme. The basic route would have involved students viewing:

Prescreens   topic screens   presentation style screens   multiple choice   topic screens   presentation style screens   multiple choice   topic screens   presentation style screens   multiple choice   exit.

The most comprehensive route would have involved:

Prescreens   topic screens   presentation style screens   presentation style screen2   multiple choice   topic screens   presentation style screens   presentation style screen2   multiple choice   topic screens   presentation style screens   presentation style screen2   multiple choice   exit

At the end of the programme students completed a one-page survey, which sought their reasons for selecting particular presentations and their perception of the usefulness of these presentations for able students and students with learning difficulties.

Findings

The students in both projects were interested and motivated in using multimedia technology. For example students registered confidence in their ability to learn with and use the Periodic CDROM and the t-test showed there was no significant change   (at $p< 0.10$ level) in students' interest, confidence and preference, after working with this particular CDROM.

The students working with the Periodic CDROM stated that they enjoyed learning with computers very much, they believed multimedia programmes were interesting and they looked forward to working with multimedia programmes. Students were also confident in their ability to learn to use a CDROM within a short duration and they believed they could retrieve useful information from the CDROM in an efficient way.

The Periodic CDROM pre project survey indicates that students were slightly inclined to learning with CDROMS as they believed that these technologies were more fun, easier and gave them more useful information, these beliefs did not change as a consequence of using the CDROM

The students believed that knowing how to use Periodic CDROMS was important for their future studies, believing they would ultimately replace textbooks. Prior to using the Periodic CDROM students did not believe that CDROMS were overloaded with information after the intervention this perception changed significantly (at $p< 0.05$).

From the data collected one would assume that these particular students held beliefs/interests that could foster positive dispositions towards independent use of CDROMS.   However, direct observation and video analysis indicated that students tended not to access unfamiliar topics. Observation and analysis also indicated that and they were most interested in the quiz section of the CDROM. Students working with the CDROM were classified according to the following categories:

- Exploratory: students accessing topics that were new to them but not quiz related activities.

- Retrospective: students accessing information that they had encountered previously.
- Quiz based: students using the quiz
- Help related: students accessing help buttons or commands.
- Unclassified: elements that did not fall into the above four categories

Less than six percent of the students total time was spent on help related or unclassified activities. Students also demonstrated a strong disposition not to access unfamiliar content. Just less than sixty percent of the total group time was spent on the quiz and only 8% of their time was spent exploring other aspects of the CDROMS.

Every student stated that the quiz was the most interesting facet of the CDROM because the game appealed. Analysis of the video tapes show that students engaged in heated debate, but while students demonstrated a disposition to discuss their ideas, they weren't disposed toward exploring the CDROM to find solutions! As a consequence they were randomly successful with their quiz responses. The quiz itself was intrinsically motivating, the content was not. The peer interaction and comparison of response was also motivating, but once again the content was not of sufficient interest to them and they did not seek assistance.

The CDROM included numerous abstract science concepts. Many of these are unlikely to be 'discovered' without suitable direction and the quiz did not provide this direction.

The video/animation study also provides more insight into student disposition with respect to working autonomously with CDROMS. For example, 16 of the 22 students followed the screen sequential presentation order to view the presentations on melting, boiling and dissolving, but 7 students indicated that they selected this order according to topic interest. During the course of the programme, 13 students said they selected a topic on the ground of perceived interest. Eleven of the 22 students viewed the initial compulsory multimedia presentations in sequential order and 9 of these students also viewed the sections on melting, boiling and dissolving in sequential order. A sizeable proportion of students either favour viewing multi-media in sequential order or are reluctant to stray from the order arbitrarily prescribed by the software. Ten students said they chose their navigational route through the software according to topic interest. The tracking evidence did not support this. On the whole, students followed the order prescribed. What is noteworthy is that students think they work autonomously, but many simply follow, albeit unconsciously, the prescribed sequential route. This is not unusual, it has long been accepted that students will work through an examination paper in presentation order without reading it through to identify which questions they are best placed to answer.

Surprisingly, students preferred viewing video footage of the macroscopic events as opposed to animations of the microscopic event, even though the macroscopic events were fairly routine, common events. (Personally I equated watching the kettle boil with the same degree of interest I have in watching paint dry.) The number of students using animations declined between selecting the first topic and selecting the second topic. Seven of the 22 students never selected animations as a presentation type. Five of these 7 students listed 'TV' or 'movies' as an interest, which may explain their preference for video as a presentation type. However the decline in selecting animation between first and second view is harder to account for. It could be that the similarity of the animations was uninspiring. Similar red and white shaped balls moving gracefully may have limited interest for those living in the computer games era, where they encounter more graphic illustrations. Or it may have been that interpreting the animated models was too much of a challenge. Making sense of white and red balls clash, vibrate and move may have been confusing.

The content of the animations (in comparison with the video clips) may have been too abstract for most students to comprehend. These animations of microscopic events are prominent in Chemistry CDROMS. In addition their understanding of what they were viewing may have lacked the necessary scaffolding; the bridge to link the abstract to what they already had stored. The majority of students signalled the need to have text. It would be easy to assume that text was an instrumental aid to their understanding, except, if that was the case student logs would show them selected between 'animations and text' or 'video and text' in equal measure. There was clearly a student preference for some form of explanation to accompany graphics in multimedia presentations. Most students identified the text explanations as being beneficial in assisting their understanding of the subject matter presented.

Students almost three-quarters of the time selected animations or video clips with text explanations. There was also a marked increased in the use of text explanations between students' selection of their first topic and second topics, but there was then a decline from the second topic to the third. Mayer (2001) also suggests that students learn better when information is concisely presented. If there is 'surplus' information then the users have limited cognitive resources to deal with the relevant information. Twenty-one of the 22 student logfiles indicated that they selected at least one presentation type with a text accompaniment at some point during the study. All 21 students said that the explanation was useful.

The log files also shows that students who did not understand the animations opted for video when given the next choice.

The 'with text' alternative for both video and animation was very popular in contrast to the version without text.

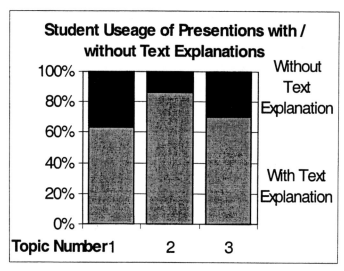

Figure 6 Student use of video or animation with or without text

The above graph representation of 'accompanying -text' versus 'no-text' presentation usage across the three topic areas of melting, boiling and dissolving (taken by students in any order, not necessarily melting, boiling and dissolving, as students may have selected boiling as their first choice instead of melting) indicates a strong preference for video/animation with accompanying text.

Ten of the students said the 'most liked' presentation format was 'video & text' and 4 students said the 'most liked' presentation format was 'animation & text'. Two students did not indicate a preference. In the student survey, 7 of the 22 students cited beneficial text explanations as a factor in selecting their 'most liked' presentation type. Five students cited 'personal interests' as their reason for choosing one presentation type ahead of another as their favourite. Two students admitted selecting their favourite presentation type according to aesthetic/ appearance properties alone.

Fifteen students nominated 'video & text' as the most helpful presentation type in assisting their understanding of the subject matter. Fourteen students cited the explanation as a reason for this. The video footage employed in the video presentations was cited as an aid to understanding by 4 of the 22 students.

One question was repeated 3 times in order to probe students' comprehension of the 3-dimensional representations of water molecules used throughout the animations. These representations are commonly found in many Chemistry CD ROMs. Five of the 22 students responded correctly on all 3 occasions. The test responses were poor for the questions relating to the molecular models used in the animations. Many students probably favoured the video presentations by default. Video was perceived to be easier to understand than animations by most of the students at this level. Many students inferred that 'good' science students would be better able to understand the animations and less likely to require the accompanying text explanation. As a consequence, they recommended that 'good' science students should try the 'no text' option as this would provide them with the necessary challenge. Weaker science students were seen as benefiting the most from a text explanation. Text may be a distraction. A number of students were observed missing important frames of animation sequences because they were reading the accompanying text. This may also account for students preferring video clips rather than animation and also account for the poor response to the multiple choice questions. The video clips were common, everyday experiments/situations that they have probably seen on numerous occasions. This may have enabled students to concentrate on reading the accompanying text while periodically viewing the screen which continued to show a kettle boiling or an ice cube melt. In contrast, the animations required continuous viewing throughout the segment, as the segments contained crucial stages. This may have resulted in difficulty if students were distracted as they read the text. For example, the crucial segment of water molecules attacking the sodium chloride lattice may have been missed while students read the explanation. Notably, the log indicates that none of the students opted to review the animation, which might indicate they were unaware that they had missed the crucial element. This would offer some support for Mayer's (2001) assertion that students learn better from animation and narration rather than animation and on screen text.

DISCUSSION

The students in both studies were motivated to use CDROMS and they believed they had the skills to use the CDROM. Yet, the Periodic CDROM project shows that they do not employ these skills to investigate the CDROM beyond the game element. Given that these students were confident in their ability to use CDROMS and their belief in the value of this technology in later life was positive, it is rather demoralising to find that when they are given free access to a well presented CDROM they focus on immediate short term gains and are drawn to the quiz. The quiz section gave them an end point, a target to aim for, and immediate feedback. They did not to review the tutorial sections in order to increase their chances of success. Their disposition toward immediate feedback may be a sign of the generation and times. The game environment of the quiz and the issue of competition, against each other or the computer, seemed to direct their use of the Periodic CDROM.

The quiz game element is basically a drill and practice exercise and it would appear that the students involved in this intervention have a disposition toward this style of information dissemination. This method of delivery may have provided the scaffolding they required but failed to find in the other sections.

Alternatively it could stem from student conditioning in established traditional classrooms where the direction to proceed is dictated consistently by the teacher. We have not fostered a culture or a disposition toward student autonomy in classroom practice. Indeed there is ample evidence of classroom talk showing that teachers hold the conversation floor and dictate the direction of classroom activity. In promoting the use of autonomous and comprehensive ICT use, perhaps we require more than the adoption of ICT in classrooms. Perhaps we need a change in our teaching and learning classroom culture. Our styles of teaching are structured to ensure that students have a predetermined closed 'end' point with immediate feedback. While we support a disposition toward an investigative style of classroom practice, we tend to dictate the direction of the investigation.

The students choice of quiz activity may be due to three factors: Circumnavigation, access to immediate goals and cognitive overload. Circumnavigation is the orientation necessary for students to repeatedly find their way to the same spot and to explore what is available without having to recall the path they took to get there should they wish to re-explore it later. The quiz was easy to find, easy to retrace and required low levels of circumnavigation. This further supports the view that students have been conditioned to be directed and led rather than lead direction. Hence in most classrooms, routes are usually mapped out for them, even if they aren't given the maps. The quiz provides immediate feedback and immediate goals. When faced with a choice of a sudden death, a ninety second challenge or a five minute challenge, all short-term goals, they showed a strong disposition toward immediacy. They all selected the sudden death option. When exploration is pursued there is a high memory demand, as students have to maintain several tasks: storing, recalling and restructuring new science concepts, recalling the pathways taken and to be taken, using technology skills (that may be new) and ensuring that the task is not mundane. The quiz section does not really require restructuring or recall of science concepts, as there is an opportunity to guess with little penalty. There is no call to ensure pathways are remembered as the quiz provides questions and the start and exit options are clear. Key boarding skills are not required as simple mouse manipulation enables the user to signal their response.

We have not encouraged a disposition toward risk taking and inquiry in our established classroom practices. Hence, it should not be surprising to find students navigating a safe, and repeatable route that incurs no penalty for creativity.

Students did not access unfamiliar topic areas, not even for a cursory glance. Multimedia has the potential to provide individual learning episodes , but without a change in the teaching and learning culture found in most classrooms, these episodes will have limited influence. Effective use of CDROMS will be limited without adequate scaffolding by the teacher and without a change in student disposition toward taking ownership of the learning process.

The Periodic CDROM project demonstrated that even when offered learner control in order to individualise learning episodes, there are some crucial aspects that need to be addressed. Student interest is a factor in determining selection choices, but the crucial aspect regarding choices appears to be how understandable, navigable, and to what extent each alternative provides instant feedback. The fact that most students selected topics in the video/animation project because they were interested in them but selected presentation style because of perceived functionality and utility in terms of learning, has ramifications for the development of CDROM materials. Simply providing students with access to good quality visual/graphic information does not result in a more learner centred learning environment as student disposition toward facets of CDROMS would indicate a preference for immediate reward, interest and perceived utility. The students taking part in the video/animation project showed a preference for video presentations, and they generally used and appreciated accompanying text explanations.

Both studies show that student navigators were not necessarily comprehensive nor were they working as effective autonomous learners. Hence though they were disposed toward using the CDROMS, they were not disposed toward using them in a way that encouraged the consideration of alternative perspectives. They were paying attention to the CDROM, they were to some extent vigilant, but they were not mindful. Students may become autonomous comprehensive navigators as their levels of experience increase and if their everyday classroom culture changes to encourage student disposition toward ownership of direction and comprehension.

Systematic use of analogical models in chemistry may promote more sophisticated understanding of chemistry. However, this systematic use will not be a consequence of leaving students to 'discover' their chemistry through interaction with a CDROM using animated analogical models. The use of these animations may simply serve to compound their concrete understanding of particles and reality. For the students involved in the study, animations had limited fruitfulness. The animation/video clip study and the Periodic CDROM study would suggest that students follow the sequence provided, they select topics according to interest, select presentation types according to utility and functionality, and select opportunities that afford them instant returns. In some cases, due to cognitive overload or navigation issues students were disposed toward the easier route (be it short term immediate response, or easily retraced pathways.) Overall, the rhetoric regarding the strengths of CDROMS will not translate into reality, unless the users of these CDROMS come to be disposed towards using the strengths found within CDROMS to enhance their learning, or if the design of the CDROMS takes into account student disposition toward games and quizzes. For, as Langer (1993) suggests, if education is not fun, then mindlessness will be found and students will miss important anomalies, and make premature cognitive commitments. How students are disposed toward accessing and interpreting information is a significant factor in the effective use of CDROMS. Students' abilities to invest in mental effort, to inquire and pursue uncertainty will distinguish between those who have cognitive ability and those whose thinking dispositions allow them to work interactively and effectively with CDROMS. The way an individual balances uncertainty, opportunity and potential catastrophe will determine to what extent they become mindful self-managing learners.

REFERENCES

Ainley, M.D., Hidi, S., & Tran, Q. (1997) *Between the lines*. Software developed in Psychology Department, University of Melbourne.

Anderson, B. (1990) Pupil's conceptions of matter and its transformation (age 12-16) *Studies in Science Education*, 18, pp. 53-85.

Atkins, M.J. (1993) Evaluating Interactive Technologies for Learning. Journal of Curriculum Studies, 25(4), pp 333-342.

Barrett, E. (1988) *Text, context and hypertext*. Cambridge, MA: MIT Press.

Beichner, R. J. (1990) The effect of simultaneous motion presentation and graph generation in a kinematics lab. *The Physics teacher,* 27, pp. 803-815.

Blumer, H (1969) Symbolic Interactionism; perspective and method. Berkley, C A University of California Press.

Bourdieu, P. (1992) *An Invitation to Reflexive Sociology.* Cambridge, Polity Press.

Brooks, H.B., & Brooks, D.W. (1996) The emerging role of CD-ROMs in teaching Chemistry. *Journal of Science Education and Teaching.* 5,(3), pp. 203-215.

Cantor, N (1990) From thought to behaviour; 'having' and 'doing' in the study of personality and cognition. *American Psychologist*, 45, 6, pp. 735-750

Cognition and Technology Group (1991) Technology and the Design of Generative Learning Environments. *Educational Technology XXXI* (5), pp. 34-39.

Costanzo, W. V (1988) Media, Metaphors and Models. *English Journal*, 77 (Nov) pp. 28-32

Cox, M. (1987) *The Effects of IT on Students' Motivation*. NCET: Coventry.

De Jong, T., & Van Joolingen, W.R. (1998) Scientific discovery learning with computer simulations of conceptual domains. *Review of Educational Research*, 68,(2), pp. 179-210.

Dillon, A., & Gabbard, R. (1998) Hypermedia as an Educational Technology: A review of the quantitative research literature on learner comprehension, control and style. *Review of Educational Research,* 68,(3), pp. 322-349.

Escalada, L.T., & Zollman, D. (1996) An Investigation on the Effects of Using Interactive Video in a Physics Classroom on Student Learning and Attitudes, *Journal of Research in Science Teaching* 34, pp. 476-489.

Fideris, J.A (1988) A grand vision. *Byte 13* (Oct) pp. 237 –244

Francis, L.J (1993) Measuring attitude toward computers among undergraduate college students: The affective domain. *Computers and Education*, 20 (3) pp. 251-255

Gardner, H. (1993) Frames of Mind: The Theory of Multiple Intelligences (Tenth Anniversary Edition). New York: BasicBooks.

Harrison, A. G., & Treagust, D. (1996) Secondary students' mental models of atoms and molecules: Implications for teaching Chemistry. *Science Education*, 80, (5), pp. 509-534.

Harwood, W.S. & McMahon, M.M. (1997) Effects of integrated video media on student achievement and attitudes in High School Chemistry, *Journal of Research in Science Teaching*, 34, 6, pp. 17-631.

Herron, J. D., & Greenbowe, T.J. (1986) What can we do about Sue? A case study of competence. *Journal of Chemical Education*, 63, (6), pp. 528-1531.

Hodson, D and Hodson, J (1998) From Constructivism to Social Constructivism: A Vygotskian Perspective on Teaching and learning Science. *School Science Review*, 79, (289), pp33-41

Johnstone, K. (1987) CLIS in the Classroom: Constructivist approaches to teaching. Education in Science, 124, pp. 129-130.

Jonassen, D. (1989) *Hypertext/hypermedia*. Englewood Cliffs, NJ: Educational technology publications.

Katz, L G (1993) Disposition as Educational Goals. ERIC Digest. Urbana IL: *Eric Clearinghouse on Elementary and Early Childhood Education*. ED 363454. Publication date 1993-09-00

Kearsley, G. (1988) Authoring considerations for hypertext. Educational Technology, 28 (11), pp. 21 –24

Kozma, R. B (1991) Learning with media. Review of Educational Research, 61(2), pp. 179-211

Kozma, R.B. (1994) Will Media Influence Learning? Reframing the Debate. Educational Technology, Research and Development 42(2), pp. 7-19.

Langer, E.J (1993) A Mindful Education. Educational Pyschologist, 28 (1) pp. 43-50

Lee, O., Eichinger, D.C., Anderson, C.W., Berkeimer, G.D. & Blakeslee, T.D. (1993) Changing middle school students' conceptions of matter and molecules. *Journal of Research in Science Teaching*, 30, pp. 249-270.

Marchionini, G. (1988) Hypermedia and learning: Freedom and chaos. Educational Technology, 28(11), pp. 8-12

Mayer, R (2001) Multimedia Learning. Cambridge: Cambridge University Press.

McCarthy, R (1989) Multimedia: What the excitement's all about. Electronic Learning 8 (Jun) pp. 26-31

McGrath, D., Cumaranatunge, C., Ji, M., Chen, H., Brace, W., & Wright, K. (1997) Multimedia Science Projects: Seven Case studies. *Journal of Research on Computing in Education*, 30, (1), pp. 18-37.

Nielsen, J. (1995) *Multimedia and hypertext: The Internet and beyond.* Cambridge, MA: Academic Press.

Park, I and Hannafin, M. J (1993) Empirically based guideline for the design of interactive multimedia. *Educational Technology Research and Development*, 47 (3) pp. 63 -65

Perkins, D., Jay, E., and Tishman, S. (1993) New Conceptions of thinking: From Ontology to Education. *Educational Pyschologist*, 28 (1) pp. 67-85

Robertson, S. L., Calder. J., Fung, P., Jones, A., and OShea, T (1995) Computer attitudes in an English secondary school. *Computers and Education* 24 (2) pp. 73 -81

Rodrigues, S., Chittleborough, G., Cirona, L., Jirik, S., Kemp, S., Sadler.J., & Bail, D. (1998) Chemistry student positions in group work involving multimedia: Students' perceptions of task and content. *Labtalk*, 42, (3), pp. 22-23.

Rodrigues, S., Chittleborough, G., Gooding, A., Papadimitropoulos, T., Varughese, V.K., Kemp, S., Sadler, J., Gilmour, M., Mckenna, B., & Helme, S. (1999) Using CD-ROMs in teaching science: findings from a small-scale study. *Australian Journal of Educational Technology,* 15, (2), pp. 1-12.

Rodrigues. S., & Wong, N. (1997) Learner access, learner control and learning: Exploring students' use of a CDROM to learn about atomic structure and periodicity. *Journal of Science and Mathematics Education in South East Asia*, XX, (1), pp. 1-12.

Shashaani, L (1993) Gender based differences in attitudes towards computers. *Computers and Education* 20 (2) pp. 169 -181

Trotter, A. (1989) Schools gear up for Hypermedia: A quantum leap in electronic learning. *American School Board Journal* 176 (Mar) pp. 35-37

Victoria Department of Education (1996) *Curriculum Standards Framework.* Melbourne, Victoria.

Von Glaserfeld, E (1995) *Radical Constructivism: A way of Knowing and Learning. Studies in Mathematics Education Series 6.* Falmer Press, Bristol, England

Vygotsky, L.S. (1934/1987) Thought and Language Cambridge, MA:MIT Press

Vygotsky, L. S. (1978) *Mind in society: The development of higher psychological processes.*

Wu, H., Krajcik, J. S. and Soloway, E. (2001) Promoting Understanding of Chemical Representations: Students' Use of a Visualisation Tool in the Classroom. *Journal of Research in Science Teaching.* 38 (7) pp. 824 – 842.

LEARNING WITH ICT: THE ROLE OF INTERACTIVITY AND STUDENT MOTIVATION

Jon Pearce and Mary Ainley

INTRODUCTION

It is generally accepted that individual students experience specific learning tasks in different ways. This is no less true for multimedia learning or learning using the internet than it is for learning using the older technologies of print and graphics. Our investigations have been designed to identify some of the patterns of individual variability that distinguish different learners. Two specific research issues are being explored in our research into students' use of ICT. The first involves investigation of ways that the interactivity possible with various forms of ICT contributes to learning. The second involves examining the detail of student motivation and engagement when ICT is used for the delivery of learning content. The methodology we are developing involves using techniques that closely monitor students' behaviour within a specific learning environment. Our intention is to use the technology as a window looking into what students are actually doing as they are engaging with (or disengaging from) particular learning content. More specifically we are asking how patterns of student reactivity are contingent on features of the medium of presentation. In short we are using some of the special features of ICT to investigate students interacting with ICT.

To set the framework for this discussion we will introduce the main issues informing our investigations. The first concerns the nature and role of interactivity in ICT. We address the general assumption that anything interactive will by definition improve learning. It is our contention that more attention could be directed to understanding what interactivity means within an ICT learning environment and that better understanding of this concept will open up a number of questions about the functions of interactivity within effective learning. The second issue that we will address concerns the role of the complex patterns of motivation that students bring with them to their learning, the specific motivation generated by the task itself, and the way these influence learning when the learning content is delivered by ICT.

1. INTERACTIVITY AND LEARNING WITH ICT

It has been a long held tenet that 'interactivity is good'. In a learning environment we accept that effective learning happens when students are interactively engaged with a learning task. We describe this under different headings such as interactivity, engagement or involvement. This belief is based, in part, on research into interactive learning using videodisc, carried out at a time before that of interactivity on the Web. Zirkin and Sumler (1994) provide a bibliography of such research and conclude that "the more interactive the instruction the more effective the learning outcome was likely to be". Najjar (1996) cites four studies (Bosco 1986; Verano 1987; Fletcher 1989; Stafford 1990) each of which examined the use of interactive videodiscs in learning and concludes that it is the increased level of interactivity which results in better learning achievement, retention of knowledge and better attitudes towards learning than traditional classroom lectures.

There is a natural assumption that this positive effect of interactivity also carries over to the kind of interactive simulations now common on the Web. This is probably a sound assumption, although we have little knowledge as to how the specific nature of such interactions supports learning. In both constructivist and social-constructivist models of learning (for a review see Salomon & Perkins, 1998), such cognitive engagement is a facet of students actively grappling with new ideas, resolving conflicts with old ideas, and constructing meaning in their own minds.

When evaluating Web-based learning we often pick up on the interactivity concept and assume that interactivity is by definition 'good' in an online learning environment. We frequently hear positive comments such as "a great learning package—highly interactive". Or critical comments such as "it lacks interaction, just electronic page-turning". Whereas such comments still appear reasonable, questions arise as to what kind of, and how much, interactivity is optimal to promote effective learning. Indeed, describing the nature of interactivity itself is not straightforward, let alone how various aspects of it affect learning.

The next section reviews some of the current ideas on the nature of interactivity. It examines the notion that interactivity can be described through four dimensions: locus of control, frequency, degrees of freedom and significance (see Graham, Pearce, Howard & Vetere, 2001), and that this perspective on interactivity helps in exploring its use in a learning context. Finally it describes techniques being used to monitor and analyse students' interactions as they progressed through a Web-based learning exercise in physics.

1.1 Meanings of Interactivity

Interactivity has held a high profile in education circles for a long time. Phrases such as 'learner centred', 'hands-on', and 'activity-based' all fit well within a constructivist philosophy of learning and imply interactivity in one form or another. This focus on interactivity has taken on an even higher profile in Web learning environments where static Web sites are often disparagingly referred to as 'electronic textbooks' which, whilst presenting valuable information, are criticised as offering nothing to engage the learner in meaningful learning tasks. The notion that for a Web-based learning environment to be effective it must be interactive, is a given for Web designers. However, defining 'interactivity' is problematic. The word takes on a range of meanings determined in part by the discipline in which it is being used and in part by the context of its use. We will examine first differences in meaning between use in both educational and design contexts.

'Interactivity' in Education Contexts

Both constructivist and social-constructivist perspectives on learning propose that learning involves the learner constructing knowledge. This happens through active participation by the learner (Salomon & Perkins, 1998; Vygotsky, 1978). The notion of 'active' versus 'passive' is crucial to this view of learning. 'Learner activity' describes the learner doing something that engages his or her mind in a task that challenges existing concepts, encourages linkages to existing concepts, or generates 'new ideas'. Existing knowledge structures or schema are modified and expanded through active engagement with the learning content. The learner is challenged to articulate their own understanding of such concepts; this is often achieved through discussing their views with others, hence refining their own views and forming conceptual links with their existing knowledge base.

The shift from being engaged in an activity by oneself, such as responding to questions or doing a science experiment alone, to carrying out an activity in conjunction with someone else, illustrates a distinction between 'activity' and '*inter*activity'. However with ICT, 'interactive' tasks allocate the role of responding partner to a computer, rather than to another person. Williams, Rice and Rogers (1988) define interactivity to include three essential components: control, exchange of roles and mutual discourse. The last component, discourse, generally used to refer to a sequence of verbal exchanges between two people, could equally well describe the exchange that occurs when a person clicks a mouse and a computer responds. Human-machine interaction is clearly an important mode for existing cognitive structures to be challenged and then modified. Stated more simply human-machine interaction is an important mode for learning.

Laurillard (1993) refers to a computer-based simulation as a medium that is interactive in the sense that it gives 'intrinsic' feedback on students' actions. This form of feedback comes naturally from the system itself, as opposed to 'extrinsic' feedback that depends on external comment from a third party. In most educational settings, provision of feedback is the role commonly adopted by the teacher. For educational material to be interactive "something in the 'world' must change observably as a result of their actions" (Laurillard 1993, p. 100). The student acts on the learning material and then observes what happens. Within a simulation a student has control. The student acts on the system and the system responds with a consequence of that action (for example, the student enters text and the system responds with text). Discourse takes place in the sense that one action causes a response that prompts a subsequent action, and so a human-machine dialogue is initiated. Interaction in this form is a valuable component of the learning process, but as Laurillard (1993) suggests this is not the complete learning process. An important omission from this description of the learning process is a strategy whereby students reflect on what they observe. Hence, the essence of interactivity, according to Laurillard, is an active learner receiving immediate feedback concerning the consequences of those actions. But equally as important is the learner perceiving or making the connection between action and consequence, between action and feedback.

Interactivity, when interpreted as an activity between people, is an extremely powerful vehicle for learning. The added value of having other humans reacting to one's thoughts and ideas helps both to challenge and reinforce developing concepts. Harrasim, Hiltz, Teles and Turoff (1995) when discussing learning networks, rate active learning incorporating collaborative learning components as the second most important factor after motivation for student success in a networked environment. The value of such collaboration is observed not only in the design of collaborative learning activities, but also in the recognition of the value of teachers in the learning process. Interactivity, in this sense, utilises direct human feedback to stimulate the reflection by students on their learning. The same interactivity can occur between machine and human. For example, a student enters parameters into a simulation and then attempts to interpret the resulting graphical output on the screen. However, it is often the close contingency between action, feedback on action, and reflection that is missing in human-computer interactions.

It is no surprise then that 'interactivity' can take on a spectrum of meanings. One end of the spectrum focuses on the task itself, the degree to which the task can engage the student and promote learning. The other end focuses on the *inter*action between one student and another (or a teacher); the interplay of minds that software of the last few decades has tried so unsuccessfully to emulate. Somewhere in between, maybe, lies a learner engaging with a computer. Hence when one refers to 'interactivity' in a Web-based learning context, one could be referring to an interaction between an individual and a computer, or an interaction between individuals mediated in some way by a computer. Both have valid places in terms of learning methodologies.

The above discussion has highlighted that a central component of the interactivity concept in educational contexts is dialogue between two or more parties. Dialogue is at the heart of the learning process.

Interactivity in Design Contexts

Exploring interactivity from a Web designer's perspective further adds to our understanding of the term. Looking for definitions of interactivity in the writings of designers quickly reveals many of the computer-human aspects of interactivity, rather than computer-human-computer aspects. This is what Szeto et al. (1997) refers to as "the components of interactivity", such as software development tools, Web environments, etc. But there is also ready acknowledgement that interactivity is ubiquitous in our world and that, in a commercial sense, computer-based interactivity has strong competition from everyday interactions. Hence to compete, an interaction designer must consider producing a "totally immersive" environment. This notion of "total immersion" applies readily, and understandably, to games and marketing Web sites where the aim is to hold the user for purposes of pleasure or sales.

A Web report by Green (1998) puts forward a taxonomy of interactivity in which he uses the term 'Immersive Media Experience' (IME). This is a broader term than 'interactive programmes' or 'multimedia programmes' because it includes the senses of touch and kinesthetics and emphasises the intense nature of these experiences. He observes that "many interactive experiences are strangely 'flat' and un-involving". He describes Csikszentmihalyi's concept of 'flow' (Csikszentmihalyi 1996) as "the state of being deeply involved in a process that offers challenges and allows a sense of achievement that results in feeling of enjoyment". Flow, he claims, is "conspicuously absent" in many IMEs. The importance of the affective side of interactivity is an observation also made by others. Laurel (1986) refers to a sense of 'first-personness' which she says is most fully realised when each of three interactive variables (frequency, range and significance) are at the extremes of their continuum. In a later book, Laurel (1991) proposes that these variables alone are not adequate to define such immersion, but that a more rudimentary measure reflects whether the user feels herself participating in the ongoing action or not (p. 20).

One message we get from the designer's viewpoint is the notion that a sense of playfulness, or 'flow', plays an important role in interactions that are designed to be engaging or immersive. If a learning site's aim is to motivate students through interactivity, then we should explore this affective side to increase the chance of success.

Applying Interactivity

Whether for the purposes of education or entertainment or commerce, it is beneficial to develop a better understanding of interactivity and how its various dimensions might be manipulated to improve the user's experience. There is no reason to assume that one ideal of optimal interactivity exists for every context of use.

In an educational context the aim might be to maximise student learning, to allow the student to manipulate the concepts and develop new links between prior knowledge and new knowledge. The degree of interactivity might be curtailed to maximize the likelihood that the student will indeed focus on the concept or the task, and in this way the educational software designer structures the learning experience. However to maximise cognitive engagement and challenge existing ideas, the nature of the interactivity needs to be carefully crafted. To do this effectively we need to know far more about student responses to particular forms of interactivity in ICT.

In contrast to education, an entertainment context might aim to engage the user in a maximal sense with a continual bombardment of outputs, user choices, and actions. The intended outcome on the user's part is enjoyment and the design for interactivity that best achieves this goal will be different to what is effective in a learning context. With yet a different purpose, a commercial context might aim to hold a user's interest in a Web site long enough to present a product or service in a way that encourages purchase or a follow-up enquiry. The interactive nature of the ICT involved might facilitate the acquisition of information that the user is seeking, or it might entice the user to accept information that she had no intention to discover. In either case, bad design will quickly lose the user to another Web site.

In order to analyse and design appropriate interactive experiences that promote learning in an educational context we need to consider the underlying dimensions of interactivity itself and this is a central focus of our investigations.

1.2 Dimensions of Interactivity

We have already seen that interactivity necessarily involves a form of dialogue. This dialogue signifies a coupling between user and system. Graham et al. (2001) regard interactivity as a dialogue having four 'dimensions': locus of control, frequency, degrees of freedom and impact of activity on dialogue. These ideas are expanded below in brief.

Locus of control refers to who is in control of the initiation, maintenance and closure of the dialogue at a point in time. The question of 'what is the balance of locus of control?' is akin to asking 'how much time does the student spend telling the computer what to do?' and 'how much time does the computer spend telling the student what to do?'. One could predict that an extreme in either direction might be detrimental in a learning context.

The second dimension, frequency, refers to how often the student is required to interact with the system. 'Interact' in this sense could mean using common input devices (mouse, keyboard, voice) to enter data, drag a slider, move an object, play a movie, click a radio button, and so on. An environment high on frequency, that requires the user to make many such interactions, could be described as 'highly interactive'. However on its own, frequency says nothing about the nature of these interactions. The next two dimensions address the nature of the interactions.

Degrees of freedom refer to the number of choices each interaction offers. Screen elements, such as radio buttons, 'next page' buttons, check boxes, each have only one degree of freedom in that they can be either on or off. A slider might have a small number of degrees of freedom, if it moves in a discrete number of steps, or it might have essentially infinite degrees of freedom if it changes a variable continuously. This notion can be extended beyond a screen element to the whole screen. A screen offering the student many choices as to what to do, click a button, move a slider, enter text, can be regarded as having many degrees of freedom. By either measure, the potential for interactivity increases as the number of degrees of freedom go up.

The fourth dimension relates to the consequence of the interaction. An interaction can be trivial in its impact on the dialogue. We say this has 'low significance'. Alternatively, it can be highly significant in that it has a major impact on the dialogue. For example, flight simulator software might allow the user to turn on and off a cockpit light with little effect on the flight. However flicking a switch that turns the engine off could be expected to have major impact, a highly significant interaction! These four dimensions are essentially orthogonal. This gives us a method for describing the interactivity of a computer-based exercise based on the value of each of these dimensions. The research described next is the beginning of a project to explore interactivity in terms of these dimensions and to investigate their effects on learning.

1.3 Monitoring Interactivity – an Experiment

As part of an ongoing investigation into how interactivity affects learning outcomes, a Web-based learning exercise (WAVES) was designed to teach how water waves from two sources interfere to produce lines referred to as 'nodes'. The material was aimed at upper secondary students or tertiary students who had not studied the topic previously. The entire exercise was Web-based and involved student survey, pre-test, learning activities, post-test and occasional probes questioning students' feelings and learning goals.

The movement of students through the site was tracked using information from Web log files. These also recorded their specific interactions within a simulation of wave interference. The students' responses to questions were collected in a separate log file and analysed.

This section describes the Web environment that students worked through and then looks at the way in which interactivity data were gathered and analysed.

Pre-Test Section

After logging in to the Web site, the first screen the students were presented with was a page asking for information about their background: age; courses studied; prior physics scores (if any); language spoken at home.

This was followed by twelve questions to gather information on the students' achievement goals (adapted from Stipek & Gralinski, 1996; Midgley, et al., 1998; Harackiewicz, Barron, Tauer, Carter & Elliott, 2000). They were asked to respond to each question using a 5-point scale from "Not at all" to "A lot". The specific dimensions measured by this scale will be described later when we consider our findings on student motivation and learning with ICT.

The next screen described the context of the learning sequence. In this case the topic was "Waves" and the context showed a bee in a pond causing water waves to radiate forming a classical "interference pattern" (see Figure 1). Students then had to respond to the question "How interesting do you expect this learning task will be?" using a five-point scale from "Not at all interested" to "Very interested". Our purpose here was to be able to investigate whether students' initial interest in the task influenced their later choices and performance.

Before starting the learning sequence, students were presented with a pre-test that tested their prior physics knowledge in this area. It comprised eight multiple-choice questions relating to water waves, wave patterns, nodes and interference.

Finally students were offered a choice between two modes to start working through the Web pages. One mode, referred to as the "static mode", let students work through Web pages that presented a structured sequence of information, much like a text book, with descriptions and images. The other mode, referred to as the "interactive mode", offered Web pages presenting a series of interactive activities with an embedded simulation to help the exploration of the specific ideas. Students' initial choice determined only their starting point. They were free to swap from the static to the interactive mode at any time during the learning sequence.

When waves meet

Introduction

You are familiar with what happens when you throw a stone into a still lake: the water is disturbed and waves spread out in increasing circles. But look at the picture below. It shows a bee disturbing water with its wings, but the wave pattern is not simply circular - it shows a series of lines radiating out from the bee.

In this exercise you will explore what those lines are, why they exist and how understanding them can be useful to us.

Now please answer the following question before proceeding:

	Not at all Interested				Very Interested
How interesting do you expect this learning task will be?	O	O	O	O	O

Figure 1

The Learning Sequence

The learning sequence comprised seven screens that students could work through in any order. In practice, most worked straight through in sequence from start to end (as was the intention). The first such screen is shown in Figure 2. At the top a navigation bar allowed students to switch from the static to the interactive modes, or to skip forwards or backwards in the sequence. At two points during the session a "probe" screen would pop up (Figure 3). This asked students about their feelings and their learning aims. This occurred the first time they changed modes (after the third screen if they hadn't changed modes) and after the sixth screen.

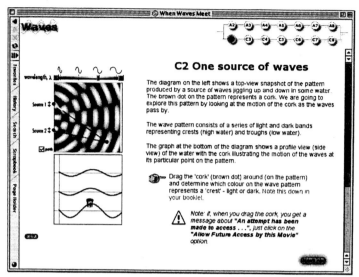

Figure 2

Figure 3

This learning sequence was designed to teach some basic ideas of how water waves interfere to form the nodes that can be observed as lines of calm water along the surface. The interactive element was a Shockwave applet that presented a view of a cork floating on the surface of water. At the left of the image was the source of the waves and this could be adjusted to become two sources. The view showed the wave patterns produced (see Figure 4). Students could vary the wavelength of the waves, adjust the separation of the two sources, turn on and off an indicator showing the path from each source to the cork, and drag the cork around the pattern. Two graphs showed the waveform from each source and a third graph showed the combined (summed) waveform at the position of the cork.

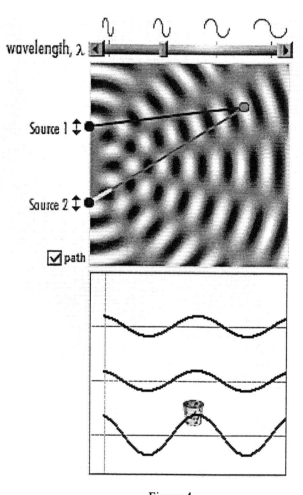

Figure 4

In the interactive mode, each screen that students worked through included an exercise that required them to interact with this applet. A question was posed in the text and interaction was required in order to answer that question. Students wrote their answers onto a worksheet. For the non-interactive mode, still images of the applet were shown with the appropriate settings to illustrate the questions posed by the text. The wording in each mode was as close as possible to the same so that the experience the students had differed only by whether or not they interacted with the applet.

Post- Test Section

On completion of the learning sequence, the students were presented with the same questions as in the pre-test (multiple-choice). Two extra questions were added that required students to type in an answer (extended-answer). These two questions were designed to assess whether students could transfer their water wave knowledge to a new situation involving sound waves.

Tracking the Students' Progress

All the information supplied on-line by students, as well as their movement through the learning site, was recorded on Web server logs. The survey data, pre and post-tests and probes were sent to a CGI script which recorded them as a time-stamped text file. This file was read into Excel, manipulated and then exported to SPSS for analysis.

All other data (pages visited and actions taken within the Shockwave applet) were recorded on the regular Web server log in a similar time-stamped format. Software was written to analyse these logs and produce numerical data of interactions as well as a visual timeline of the activities of each student.

Figure 5 shows the output from the interactivity analysis for one student's session. The display is a timeline with the upper half of the graph showing boxes representing visits by the student to static pages; the lower part showing boxes representing visits to interactive pages. Each successive page through the learning sequence is represented by a box positioned further away from the central horizontal time-axis of the plot. This particular student first visited three interactive pages, jumped to the static equivalent of the third page, then continued on interactively for two more pages, jumped to a static page again, back to interactive, and so on.

This time-line view of a student's movement through the learning materials gives us a glimpse of strategies they might employ to assist their learning. At a coarse level, we can identify those who work straight through the interactive pages from start to finish, those that follow the static path, and those that skip from one to the other. For example, figure 5 shows a pattern that looks as if the student has chosen the interactive path but is cross-checking to see that they are 'getting' it. It was fairly common to see patterns like this indicating students taking a quick peek at the other mode to check that they were not missing out on anything of value. The validity of this interpretation can only be checked by interviewing the students after the session.

The triangular markers on the lower part of the graph indicate discrete interactive events, that is, changing settings in the simulation (wavelength, source separation, path difference display). The shaded bands indicate the continuous interactive event of dragging the cork. More detailed statistics were made available as a text output file.

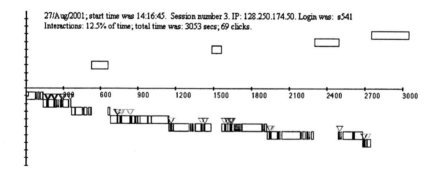

Figure 5

1.4 Discussion

Analysing the impact of interactivity within this study is part of an ongoing investigation. However, an analysis of data thus far indicates directions for future work.

Students were given a free choice as to which mode to work in: static, interactive or mixed. Of the 118 students undertaking the study, about 19%

worked through the static, textbook-like pages without referring to the interactive screens at all. This in itself is interesting in that not all students were attracted by the "lure" of interactivity. Just over half (54%) stayed entirely with the interactive screens, while the remaining 26% visited both types of pages, often following mainly the interactive pages, with occasional visits to the "other side".

An initial exploration of how these factors impact learning was carried out by defining "learning improvement" as being the arithmetic difference between post-test and pre-test. For the students following a purely interactive path there was a strong relationship between the number of clicks they used and their learning improvement. The number of clicks essentially indicated the amount of interactivity in that it counted the number of pages visited, how many times the cork was dragged around the wave pattern, and number of times the settings of the simulation were altered (wavelength, number of sources, path difference display). The amount of time spent dragging the cork actually related in a negative sense to the learning improvement. This suggests that we might be seeing the effect of learning strategies at work: excessive dragging of the cork might indicate non-strategic exploration and not contribute to learning outcomes. This might reflect a less significant form of interaction. On the other hand, clicking frequently changed the very pattern that students were viewing. This is a highly significant change to the simulation and may involve a more strategic approach to their exploration.

Further research is required to determine the substance of such strategies. Future groups of students will undertake the task in a usability lab where their behaviour can be videoed. In addition interviews, where students are asked to reflect on what they have been doing, will help us better understand their strategies and reasoning.

2. MOTIVATION AND LEARNING WITH ICT

One of the strategies we have adopted for assessing the impact of ICT on student learning is to consider its contribution to motivational processes that represent ways students engage with a task, and that ultimately influence learning. One of the most common claims supporting the use of ICT in educational contexts is that ICT enhances student motivation. Our investigations have included a number of motivational dimensions and we have examined how these dimensions contribute to the impact of specific ICT characteristics on student learning.

Some motivational research focuses on general orientations that continue over time (e.g., Ames, 1992; Dweck & Leggett, 1988; Hidi & Harackiewicz, 2000; Pintrich, 2000). Other researchers (e.g., Hidi, 1990; Hidi & Berndorff, 1998) direct attention to motivational states that are active at a specific point in time. In our studies we have included variables to represent both general and specific levels of student motivation. At the level of general motivational orientations we have concentrated on students' achievement goals, the pattern of goals that describes their general response to achievement situations. At the specific task level we have included measures of topic interest and specific task goals to determine what particular motivational factors are influencing both involvement and performance.

Achievement Goal Orientations

From the standpoint of general motivational orientations the most widely researched variables are achievement goal orientations (see Ames, 1992; Dweck & Leggett, 1988; Hidi & Harackiewicz, 2000; Pintrich, 2000). In this literature a major distinction is drawn between mastery goals and performance goals. Mastery goals are operating when students are trying to understand new information, when they want to improve personal competence. On the other hand, performance goals are operating when students focus on seeking positive evaluations of their ability and performance. Sometimes the positive evaluation of performance is through the recognition that comes with public acknowledgment of achieving high grades (wanting to do well, to be top of the class). Sometimes it is through the ego-enhancement that goes with achievement (wanting to better than other students). In some of the recent research in this area a further distinction is being made between performance goals that represent a positive approach to achievement and others that represent goals of wanting to achieve in order to avoid failure (see Barron & Harackiewicz, 2001). Such goals may implicate an important social reference group that the student does not want to disappoint (wanting to do well so as not to let down family or friends), or, does not want to lose face with peers (wanting to do well so I don't look stupid). Another achievement goal orientation sometimes included in this literature has been described as work avoidance where the goal is to get by with the minimum of effort.

These achievement goal orientations have been used widely and have been shown to be associated with students' responses to different types of classroom environments, whether students choose challenging tasks, and their degree of involvement in learning (Ames & Archer, 1988; Harackiewicz & Elliot, 1993).

Generally mastery goals have been associated with stronger learning outcomes. The picture with performance goals is more complex. Early writers focused on the negative or maladaptive consequences of performance goals. However, as was suggested in an early model proposed by Dweck (1986) students' confidence in their own competence influences the way in which learning is affected by performance goals. When a student is unsure of their own competence, or they perceive the task to be difficult, performance goals are likely to be associated with poorer performance. When confidence is higher performance goals are more likely to be associated with positive learning outcomes. However, as more and more studies are being conducted in this area the factors that influence relationships between students' achievement goals and learning are being identified (see Hidi & Harackiewicz, 2000 for a review). In our investigations we are particularly concerned to identify how achievement goals as general orientations influence what happens in specific ICT learning environments and so we included a measure of achievement goals orientation assessing students' mastery, performance, and work avoidant goals.

Topic Interest

In our investigations a key indicator of specific motivation has been measurement of the level of interest in the topic when it is first presented. We have been concerned to identify what motivation has been triggered by the particular learning task. At the point in the software where the physics problem was first described the student was asked to rate how interesting they expected it to be. We have considered this to be a measure of topic interest. A number of sources contribute to the level of topic interest. For example, students who have a general interest in science will be more likely to respond with elevated levels of topic interest as the learning task is a specific problem in physics (e.g., Hoffmann & Haussler, 1998). In addition, features of the way in which the topic or problem is introduced may arouse interest in students not otherwise generally interested in physics. With our particular software inclusion of the photograph of the bee on the pond and the unexpected pattern of lines in the water might be expected to trigger student interest. The general expectation is that when higher topic interest is triggered students will become more involved in the task and so show higher performance on measures of learning outcomes.

Specific Task Goals

One of the enduring issues for the study of motivation and learning is how and under what conditions general dispositions or orientations are expressed in what students do in specific situations. For our investigations this concerns the conditions that see general achievement goals translated into the actual goals being pursued with a specific problem. As described earlier we have developed 'probes' that require a quick response from students indicating the specific goals they are pursuing at a designated point as they work through the information about the physical properties of waves. The same probes include a number of emotion terms that we are investigating along with the specific task goals.

Measurement of these general and specific motivational variables provides a way of identifying how students' motivation contributes to learning with ICT. We now turn to look at some specific findings and will describe some of the relationships we have found between general achievement goals and learning using ICT.

2.1 Achievement Goal Orientations and Learning With ICT

The findings reported here are from students who were first year undergraduate Psychology students. Most were not studying physics. Therefore at the outset it needs to be stated clearly that the patterns we are reporting need to be supplemented with data from students who have more specialist experience studying physics. Students' past experience with physics studies was included to control for any effects of background familiarity with the discipline. The scores from both the multiple-choice and the extended-answer assessments of learning, not unexpectedly, were related to students' prior experience with learning physics. Students who had some physics experience beyond general secondary science performed significantly better on both types of test than did students without specific physics experience.

After allowing for differences in students' prior physics experience it was found that achievement goal orientation influenced learning as assessed by both measures of achievement in the WAVES program. Mastery goals were positively related to learning. Higher levels of mastery goals were associated with higher scores on both the multiple-choice and the extended-answer questions. On the other hand, performance goals were negatively related to both indicators of learning. Students with higher performance goals were likely to have lower scores on both measures of learning. Specific patterns of association linking mastery goals and learning as found in our first study using WAVES will now be described in more detail.

2.2 MASTERY GOALS AND LEARNING: SOME MEDIATING PROCESSES

There was a complex sequence of reactions that linked students' mastery goals and their learning scores. In addition, there were some important differences between the processes that were implicated in the sequences linking mastery goals and the two types of learning. First, consider again some of the specific variables monitored in the WAVES program.

Topic Interest

After completing the questions dealing with their general approaches to learning (achievement goal orientations), students were presented with a photograph of a bee on a pond of water. The flapping of the bee's wings was creating two sets of waves and the pattern that could be seen was clearly not the expected set of concentric circles normally seen when a stone is dropped into a pond of water. The problem was posed in terms of understanding how to explain this wave pattern. Students were first asked to indicate using a five-point Likert-type scale, how interesting they expected the learning program to be. This rating provided an index of the interest that had been triggered by the topic to be learned, here referred to as topic interest.

Presentation Mode.

To start on the learning material students had to choose one of two paths, the static, textbook-on-the-screen version of the learning material or the interactive version. The interactive version presented the same material as the static version. However, instead of having graphics depicting what happened under conditions of different wavelengths and different distances between the wave sources, this version included the Shockwave applet that allowed students to independently control important dimensions such as wavelength and distance between wave sources. They could then observe any changes to the character of the waves at the point of the cork floating on the water. After choosing which version they wanted to start with, students were free to switch between the static and interactive modes. The initial screen choice and all of the movements between screens were monitored and the pattern of activity coded to represent the main way the material had been accessed. Students who chose one mode and stuck with that (or made minimal forays into the other mode), were classified as either *textbook* or *interactive* depending on which they chose. Students who changed a number of times between these two modes were classified as *mixed*.

Cognitive Strategies.

The final step in the WAVES program was a short questionnaire that asked students to report on the specific strategies they had used while working through the program. The items had been used in previous research where students had been asked to report on strategies used in preparing for examinations (Ainley, 1993; Thomas & Bain, 1984), and studying during a semester long course (Harackiewicz et al., 2000). In the present study they were to respond in terms of the specific task just completed. The items were designed to distinguish deep strategies from surface strategies. Deep strategies, sometimes called elaborative or transformational strategies, involve students trying to understand the meaning of new information. They involve linking new information with previous knowledge, and in general constructing a meaningful system out of the new information. Surface strategies, sometimes called reproductive strategies, involve students trying to remember as much of the new information as they can in its present form. The essence of this type of strategy is summed up in the item asking students how much they tried to 'learn the material off-by-heart'. Hence, it was possible to include an indication of the level that students used these two types of cognitive strategy when learning about what happens when waves from two sources meet.

From Mastery Goals to Learning.

In the first analyses of these data relationships between prior physics experience, achievement goal orientation, topic interest, engagement, cognitive strategies and learning outcomes have been modelled (see Peachy, 2001). The statistical significance for all relationships presented here were tested using multiple regression analyses.

For the multiple-choice retention measure of learning (shown in Figure 6), mastery goals; goals of understanding, improving competence and skills, were linked to achievement through students use of deep cognitive strategies. Students with higher mastery goals tended to report more use of deep cognitive strategies. More use of deep cognitive strategies when learning the new information about waves, was associated with higher scores on the multiple-choice retention test. This effect of mastery goals was in addition to the effect of prior physics experience on learning outcome.

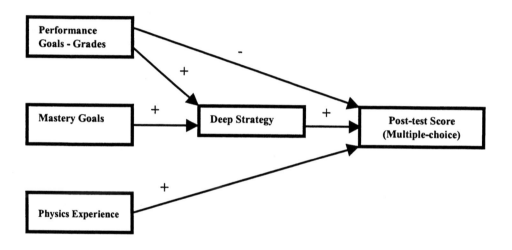

Figure 6

For the extended –answer or questions requiring transfer of knowledge to a new situation, mastery goals worked through different processes (see Figure 7). In this case higher mastery goals influenced learning through the triggering of more interest in the topic. Students with higher topic interest were more likely to choose the interactive learning path and this in turn was associated with higher learning scores. These data suggest that mastery goals influenced the specific processes that were called into play when students interacted with new material. Of particular significance for our understanding of the ways that ICT might impact on learning was the finding that mastery goals and the interest triggered by the topic itself influenced learning when students chose the interactive learning mode.

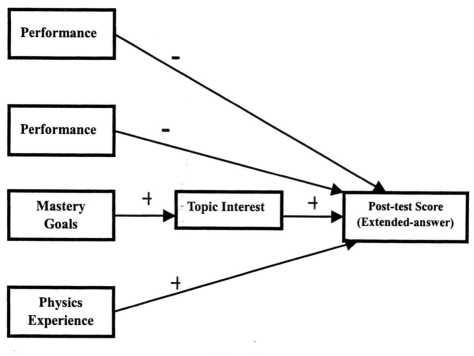

Figure 7

What does this mean? Students who want to increase their understanding of a topic, and who have had their general mastery orientation focussed by the interest triggered in the specific learning task, learnt more effectively when they had some active part in the learning. So what is the process? Although by no means definitive, these findings suggest that a crucial part of the effectiveness of interactivity in ICT is whether the student wants to understand the new information. Theories of interactivity stress the 'active' learner who builds their knowledge by receiving feedback on the consequences of their planned actions. A crucial element in this formula for learning would seem to be the planned activity, the testing and re-testing relationships possible through the interactive mode. Access to the interactive mode allows the student to get into the problem and more powerful learning results.

From Performance Goals to Learning.

Students' performance goals showed a different relationship with learning. Students who endorsed performance goals were concerned to do well. They wanted to score well on the test. Some of the reasons behind this strong desire to perform well are found in the positive feedback that doing well on the test gives students about their own ability level. Standards of performance are important. They want to be known for doing well. Sometimes this has been described in terms of performing to please family and friends. A preliminary check on the factor structure of the achievement goal items that students answered suggested that the students who participated had two separate bases for responses to the performance goal orientation items. With samples from the United States where these measures have been developed, two sets of performance goals have been described as performance-approach and performance-avoidance. In our data the distinction within the performance goal statements was between performing to get good grades and performing for social reasons such as meeting the expectations of family and friends or to outperform other students. In Figures 6 and 7 these have been labelled Performance Goals–Grades, and Performance Goals-Social.

In the research literature performance goals have shown equivocal findings. In some studies higher performance goals have been associated with poor achievement, in other studies higher performance goals have been associated with higher achievement (see Hidi & Harackiewicz, 2000 for a review). In some of the early work on performance goals reported by Dweck (1986) it was suggested that performance goals do not promote strong learning when students' assessment of their competence is low. The data presented here were obtained from students most of whom had not studied physics. We found that performance goals were negatively related to scores on both measures of learning, multiple-choice questions and extended-answer questions (see Figures 6 and 7). As mentioned earlier we distinguished between two types of performance goals; concern over getting good grades and concern over social comparisons and expectations. For these students it was the performance goal based on a concern to get good grades, or to do well on the test, that was significantly related to the learning outcomes. Given the students' relative inexperience with physics this finding is consistent with Dweck's theory that performance goals are not associated with strong learning when students' assessment of their own competence is low.

A more complex pattern emerged when the relationships between the variables and scores on the multiple-choice test of learning were considered. As can be seen in Figure 6 there was a positive association between performance goals and learning scores when those performance goals were combined with students adopting deep strategies in their learning. Students who were concerned about getting good grades and who adopted strategies that involved linking ideas together, that is, deep or transformational strategies, were likely to gain higher scores on the test.

In summary, the specific patterns of goals, intentions and purposes that students bring to their learning have important influences on individual responses to the learning task. This is no less the case when the learning mode involves ICT. Part of the expanded learning opportunities claimed for ICT involve specific learning features that are likely to be taken up to different degrees by different students. An interactive module within a well designed learning sequence will only support learning if students actually engage with it, if they are active in changing parameters and observing consequences in the phenomenon being displayed. Not all students come to their learning with goals and purposes compatible with this learning mode.

The results reported here are not exhaustive and this is still best described as "work in progress". However, we are encouraged to find that our results are generally consistent with the findings reported from other research programs (e.g., Mayer, 1997; Mayer, Moreno, Spires & Lester, 2000) that are currently investigating the processes that contribute to effective learning with ICT.

REFERENCES

Ainley, M.D. (1993) Styles of engagement with learning: Multidimensional assessment of their relationship with strategy use and school achievement. *Journal of Educational Psychology*, 85, pp. 395-405.

Ames, C. (1992) Classrooms: Goals, structures, and student motivation. *Journal of Educational Psychology*, 84, pp. 261-271.

Ames, C., & Archer, J. (1988) Achievement goals in the classroom: Students' learning strategies and motivation processes. *Journal of Educational Psychology*, 80, pp. 260-267.

Barron, K.E., & Harackiewicz, J.M. (2001) Achievement goals and optimal motivation: Should we promote mastery, performance, or both types of goals? *Journal of Personality and Social Psychology*, 80, pp. 706-222.

Bosco, J. (1986) An analysis of evaluations of interactive video. *Educational Technology*, 25, pp. 7-16.

Csikszentmihalyi, M. (1996) *Creativity, flow and the psychology of discovery and invention*, Harper Collins.

Dweck, C.S. (1986) Motivational processes affecting learning. *American Psychologist,* 41, pp. 1040-1048.

Dweck, C.S., & Leggett, E.L. (1988) A social-cognitive approach to motivation and personality. *Psychological Review*, 95, pp. 256-273.

Fletcher, D. (1989) The effectiveness and cost of interactive videodisc instruction. *Machine-Mediated Learning,* 3, pp. 361-385.

Graham, C., Pearce, J., Howard, S. & Vetere, F. (2001) *Levels of interactivity and interactivity maps. OzCHI 2001.* Fremantle, Australia.

Green, J. S. (1998) *A taxonomy of interactivity.* Carat International.

Harackiewicz, J. M., & Elliot, A. J. (1993) Achievement goals and intrinsic motivation. *Journal of Personality and Social Psychology*, 65, pp. 904-915.

Harackiewicz, J.M., Barron, K.E., Tauer, J.M., Carter, S.M. & Elliot, A.J. (2000) Short-term and long-term consequences of achievement goals in college: predicting continued interest and performance over time. *Journal of Educational Psychology*, 92, pp. 316-330.

Harrasim, L., S. R. Hiltz, et al. (1995) *Learning Networks.* Cambridge, Massachusetts, The MIT Press.

Hidi, S. (1990) Interest and its contribution as a mental resource for learning. *Review of Educational Research*, 60, pp. 549-571.

Hidi, S., & Berndorff, D. (1998) Situational interest and learning. In L. Hoffmann, A. Krapp, & K. A. Renninger (Eds.), *Interest and learning: Proceedings of the Seeon Conference on interest and gender* (pp. 74-90). Kiel, Germany: IPN.

Hidi, S., & Harackiewicz, J. (2000) Motivating the academically unmotivated: A critical issue for the 21st century. *Review of Educational Research*, 70, pp. 151-179.

Hoffmann, L. & Haussler, P. (1998) An intervention project promoting girls' and boys' interest in physics. In L. Hoffmann, A. Krapp, K. A. Renninger, & J. Baumert (Eds.), *Interest and learning: Proceedings of the Seeon Conference on interest and gender* (pp. 301-316). Kiel, Germany: IPN.

Laurel, B. (1986) Interfaces as mimesis. In D. A. Norman & S. Draper.(Eds.) *User centered system design: New perspectives on human-computer interaction.* Hillsdale, NJ: Lawrence Erlbaum.

Laurel, B. (1991) *Computers as theatre.* Reading: Addison-Wesley.

Laurillard, D. (1993) *Rethinking University Teaching.* London, Routledge.

Mayer, R.E. (1997) Multimedia learning: Are we asking the right questions? *Educational Psychologist*, 32, pp. 1-19.

Mayer, R.E., Moreno, R., Spires, H.A., & Lester, J.C. (2000) The case for social agency in computer-based teaching: Do students learn more deeply when they interact with animated pedagogical agents? *Paper presented at the Annual Meeting of the American educational Research Association*, New Orleans, April.

Midgley, C., Kaplan, A., Middleton, M., Maehr, M.L., Urdan, T., Anderman, L., Anderman, E., & Roeser, R. (1998) The development and validation of scales assessing students' achievement goal orientations. *Contemporary Educational Psychology*, 23, pp. 113-131.

Najjar, L. J. (1996) Multimedia information and learning. *Journal of Educational Multimedia and Hypermedia*, 5(2), pp. 129-150.

Peachy, T. (2001) *Goal orientation, topic interest and learning style preferences of students with a web delivered task.* Unpublished Honours thesis, University of Melbourne.

Pintrich, P. R. (2000) An achievement goal theory perspective on issues in motivation terminology, theory and research. *Contemporary Educational Psychology*, 25, pp. 92-104.

Salomon, G., & Perkins, D.N. (1998) Individual and social aspects of learning. *Review of Research in Education*, 23, pp.1-24.

Stafford, J. Y. (1990) *Effects of active learning with computer-assisted or interactive video instruction.* Detroit, Wayne State University.

Stipek, D., & Gralinski, J.H. (1996) Children's beliefs about intelligence and school performance. *Journal of Educational Psychology*, 88, pp. 397-407.

Szeto, G. M.,Butterick, M., Spenser, J., Harlan, D., Karam, D., Vanuti, S., Beach, D., Bugaj, S., Tackenberg, R., & Merholz P. (1997) *Designing interactive web sites.* Indianapolis: Hayden Books.

Thomas, P.R., & Bain, J.D. (1984) Contextual dependence of learning approaches: The effects of assessments. *Human Learning*, 3, pp. 227-240.

Verano, M. (1987) *Achievement and retention of Spanish presented via videodisc in linear, segmented and interactive modes.* University of Texas.

Vygotsky, L. S. (1978) Mind in society. Cambridge: Harvard University Press.

Williams, F., R. E. Rice & Rogers, E. M. (1988) *Research methods and the new media.* New York: Collier Macmillan Publishers.

Zirkin, B. G. & Sumler, D. E. (1994) "Interactive or non-interactive?: That is the question!!" *Journal of Distance Education.* 10(1).

INDEX

W

Z